ART 2 START

Startup Shastra: A 15 Sutra Entrepreneurship MBA

Sandeep Mehndiratta

INDIA • SINGAPORE • MALAYSIA

Notion Press Media Pvt Ltd

No. 50, Chettiyar Agaram Main Road,
Vanagaram, Chennai, Tamil Nadu – 600 095

First Published by Notion Press 2021
Copyright © Sandeep Mehndiratta 2021
All Rights Reserved.

ISBN 978-1-63850-838-0

This book has been published with all efforts taken to make the material error-free after the consent of the author. However, the author and the publisher do not assume and hereby disclaim any liability to any party for any loss, damage, or disruption caused by errors or omissions, whether such errors or omissions result from negligence, accident, or any other cause.

While every effort has been made to avoid any mistake or omission, this publication is being sold on the condition and understanding that neither the author nor the publishers or printers would be liable in any manner to any person by reason of any mistake or omission in this publication or for any action taken or omitted to be taken or advice rendered or accepted on the basis of this work. For any defect in printing or binding the publishers will be liable only to replace the defective copy by another copy of this work then available.

Recommendation

"Art 2 Start" provides a simple yet thorough step-by-step strategy that will help individuals develop an entrepreneurial mindset. Sandeep does a brilliant job of articulating various startup fundamentals by drawing upon his years of experience in the entrepreneurship arena. The theme of this book is extremely relevant in current times as we continue to witness an explosion in innovation and the need to deliver sustained customer value. An insightful book for both budding entrepreneurs and professionals alike.

– Vipin Sondhi (MD & CEO Ashok Leyland, India)

A crisply written book that provides great tool-kit for any start-up with simple but innovative approach that not only guides but also inspires.

It is exciting to see interesting use of concepts like 5S, GOD, ASK, CLOVE to build one's perspective towards designing solutions.

"Start-o-meter" is another innovative and powerful self-assessment tool for start-ups. Sandeep has comprehensively condensed key elements of an entrepreneur's journey in to "Start-up Shastra".

A must-read for the ones who want to give wings to their dreams.

– Sanjeev Arora (Chief Technology Officer, JCB India Head Quarters)

Dedication

I dedicate this meager effort to my loving father who was my friend, my guru, my everything. He was the one who gave me wings. I cherish memories of his life lessons and stories of wisdom that were full of zeal. He was an inspiration to many and had a will-power of steel. He wanted me to publish this book but I could not do this in front of his eyes. I laid him down to rest and missed his pat, when I fall and needed to rise. I was down, shattered and low, with no aspirations and nowhere to go. I gathered my strength to recall his vision for society, the mindfulness and optimism to see every risk as an opportunity.

I have a promise to make, I'll ask myself daily when I wake.
I am on a mission to make you proud of your son,
Your dreams are mine and second to none.
We are separated by death but together by love,
I know, you are blessing me from far above…

I bow down to the wholehearted support of my mom and my spouse to complete the book. And of course, special thanks to my loving daughters, Bhakti and Khushi, for numerous proofreads.

Preface

"Entrepreneur", the word itself is so inspiring and captivating that we fall in love for being one. This book is for challengers who are seeking an answer to either of the four questions:

   a. I want to start, but what, how, and where to start?
   b. I already have an idea, how can I build conviction & a business model?
   c. I am a professional in a job, can an entrepreneurial mindset help me?
   d. I am in the middle of my career, can I start something now?

Most engineers while graduating have a dream of starting something new to change the world. The excitement to solve a problem is at the highest level. This is the time when a passionate idea is challenged by the economics of the business and creates a dichotomy between mind and heart. Heart says… "Go for it", but a cautious mind wants to wait and study the idea. Few people are bold enough to follow their dream, while others wait for a more opportune time. An entrepreneurial mindset has conviction in ideas and clarity in the business model.

Entrepreneurship is about living one's passion and eventually, it becomes a profession. They are driven by a dream to do something transformational for themselves

PHASE 1

Getting in the Groove

1

A Day with DAREDEVIL

*There are no born Entrepreneurs
Vision nurtures them, Ideas build them,
Skills strengthen them and Values shape them*

– SMR

Engineers perceive themselves as beings who could understand almost any topic in the world, analyze it like a supercomputer, and give away precise advice on it. The last thing an engineer would like to

hear is about cleaning up his messed-up room. If you have seen a hostel room, it is evident that clothes, stationery, instruments and even important documents are flying freely but don't know where these things suddenly disappear when we need them the most.

It was 2006, a good 5 years since I had graduated in production engineering. I was proudly carrying these habits from my hostel days but never used to boast about it. During these 5 years, I had changed 5 companies, worked in 7 different job profiles, scrapped a couple of start-up ideas, and had got married once. I was then in a full-time job, leading engineering department of a multi-national company, "CLAAS", engaged in manufacturing Harvester Combines (*agricultural equipment*) at Faridabad, in India.

Earlier, I always used to think that an Idea is everything for a startup. Hence my initial ideas were good on paper only as practical implementation is a different ball game altogether. No doubt, Ideas are key but it is more important to connect with the real problem. The power of an idea is proportional to the extent to which it can solve a problem by either killing pain or creating gain.

I was about to learn these lessons and the learning journey was initiated with an industry expert who then joined as my boss.

The Countdown Begins

It was the month of July when the sound of thundershowers woke me up early that day. The first monsoon drizzle had suddenly switched the hostile hot climate to a pleasant one.

I could feel the positivity and excitement of a rainy day although, I was more excited to meet my new boss who had taken charge as plant head. I already had lost some time, so got ready in a jiffy, had my breakfast, and got inside the car to head for the office in sharp 20 minutes; that's the maximum time an engineer needs for his daily morning chores.

As I walked into the office, I could sense positive energy in all my colleagues. Soon it turned into anxiety when I got a message that my new boss wanted to meet me. In a few minutes, I was sitting in front of him in his cabin along with two of my colleagues, Animesh and Vinny, who were from Fabrication and Assembly functions. We could feel the strong winds of change, partially due to the thundering weather and also due to the new seemingly strict boss.

The new boss, Mr. Nayak, in his mid-40s was a short-haired person with a rectangular wheatish face, brown sparkling eyes, raised eyebrows at 30^0, and a nicely trimmed mustache with clearly defined pointed ends. He looked like a tiger on a mission. After our formal introduction, he was quick to get on to the business.

He started talking about the fundamentals of lean manufacturing. I was familiar with these concepts and had practiced these in my earlier organizations hence I knew that "Lean" makes things simpler and removes waste. The underlying statement for Lean is "More in less" i.e. more output with the less or same level of inputs.

Mr. Nayak wanted to understand the manufacturing process from us and how "Lean" the process was?

My two colleagues were trying their best to impress him by answering his curiosities. After a while I could see the stress behind their smiling faces "Sir, material moves from here to here and then goes there", Animesh explained by drawing up a flow chart on a white sheet.

"Guys, hear me out...you are repeatedly giving me the same answer, my question is", "how lean is this process", Mr. Nayak asked. "Sir, this is the best process and we are using lesser resources than last year to manufacture the same components" explained Vinny by opening both palms of his hands.

Suddenly, Vinny realized that he was gesturing with all 10 fingers awkwardly towards Mr. Nayak. He immediately started closing back his fingers into fists, and bought his arms back down to his sagging sides to adjust his pants. I had started to lose my attention and finally took a sigh of relief when I saw the office boy knocking at his door with some *masala* tea.

Mr. Nayak seemed a bit impatient as he was not getting what he wanted to know. I didn't want to disturb the process champions hence I kept cool and focused on masala tea.

Finally, he asked me, "*Agar apki chai ho gayi ho toh* (if you are done with your tea), can you share your opinion on the process". I replied, "Sir, Let's have a plant round first, "Gemba" would simplify the understanding of the process".

"**Gemba**" is a Japanese term that means "the real place". Going to the "Gemba" broadens the perspective and the real scenario is experienced. "Gemba" approach ensures the **focus is on the process and not on the perception**.

We took Mr. Nayak through all the processes in manufacturing and he was quick to take some notes in his diary and it seemed like he was preparing a red diary of our sins.

After the plant round, he shared his observations:

1. The Assembly area was poorly organized
2. Cleanliness and safety were poor

He said there were a few more issues but we need to first address the top 2 as these were the **real core problems**

Vinny pointed out that it was a German plant and we had the best in class processes and there were no real problems. It seemed like a shy cat had challenged a hungry Tiger. Before Mr. Nayak could respond, I could not stop myself from sharing GOD's approach.

> *"Look at processes from a clean slate perspective, you will see problems. Look at problems from GOD's perspective, you will see solutions"*
>
> *– SMR*

I could see an instant spark in Mr. Nayak's eyes and he asked me to share this in detail. I added, "We should look at processes without any past baggage or pre-conceived notions. This would help us to spot problems. Then see problems from GOD's perspective, we would see solutions. Now, let us first understand **GOD**"

- **G**enerator (Brahma)
- **O**perator (Vishnu)
- **D**estroyer (Mahesh)

    a. **Generator**: means what generates the problem i.e. **root cause.** The problem would be visible but the root cause might be hidden
    b. **Operator:** Then, how it gets carried across processes i.e. **support system** of the problem, and
    c. **Destroyer:** Then, think how it can be **eliminated**

The focus should be to eliminate the root cause and or cut the support system. GOD's perspective is a very unique way of looking at the problem and its **REAL** root cause.

Mr. Nayak wanted us to study and validate his observations. He told us to divide the areas between the three of us and give him a high-level report on improvement opportunities.

We happily said. "Sure Sir, Definitely Sir". I knew three of us were thinking on the same line…"It's lunchtime now, let's catch up in the evening to decide, what to do and how to do".

As we were about to step out of his cabin, he bowled us with a yorker, "It is 1 'O clock now, and can we see the report by 4". Without thinking, there came a prompt reply from our fast bowler, Animesh, "Sure Sir, Sure". Vinny too followed it with a bouncer by saying, "Absolutely Sir, we should do it today only". As if all were testing their bowling skills at the tail-ender and I was left with no option but to follow the stream hence I just nodded, almost saying…SURE

For the first time, I could see a positive competition amongst friends. Soon, we had the first working lunch of our lives where we discussed processes and performance instead of bizarre start-ups, booze, and bar. We planned to develop the report by 4. We studied the identified processes, analyzed the gaps, and prepared a high-level report.

Finally, we got a pat on the back in the evening by Mr. Nayak, who concluded that our report and his observations point towards a strong business case for Workplace Organization.

Entrepreneurship Takeaways

- Breakthrough ideas germinate when an entrepreneur experiences the real issue on the actual playing field. Hence, **Gemba,** the real place, is the first step to experience the gravity of real issues
- I could relate GOD's perspective with over a couple of start-up ideas which I had to scrap. I was always curious to quickly get on to Ideas for implementation but had failed to have a laser-sharp focus on:

  a. The **real problem**
  b. Looking at the problem from **GOD's perspective**

  We tend to beat around the bush diluting the real core issues. The testimony of the real problem is that, when if resolved, would create a real value for the customer.

- Drill down issue using GOD's perspective i.e. the root cause, support system, and elimination technique

2

Three Layered Sandwich

> *There is something that is much more scarce,*
> *Something finer far, something rarer than ability.*
> *It is the ability to recognize ability.*
>
> *– Elbert Hubbart*

In the next couple of days, everyone was guessing that something new and big was going to come. Mr. Nayak ended all rumors in the morning meeting by announcing a company-wide drive on "Workplace Organization", also known as 5S.

5S is a Japanese concept for organizing a workplace. It is an acronym, where each "S" is named after a Japanese term i.e.

1. Seiri *means* SORT
2. Seiton *means* SET IN ORDER
3. Seiso *means* SHINE
4. Seiketsu *means* STANDARDISE
5. Shitsuke *means* SUSTAIN

I was not at all interested in learning Japanese but I had crammed these alien words to answer any queries *(these jargons help a lot during job interviews)*.

Mr. Nayak concluded the meeting by saying, "We will be forming a 5S core team and the team selection would be purely based on '**Three Layered Sandwich**'

Everyone was then curious about the 'Three Layered Sandwich' concept and we ran to our systems after the meeting. Animesh assumed, "It would be three rounds of an interview where he would grind us like black pepper to sprinkle on his sandwich"

Then came a wining voice, "Mil Gaya..." *(got it)*

Vinny exclaimed, "I found it on Google" and as he clicked the link, we heard a very grinning voice from him,

"Sorry guys, that's a recipe for a three-layered sandwich, you need cheese, potatoes, and onions".

Even "Google" uncle, could not help us.

It looked like only one man in this world knew this concept and he had his terminology and way of doing things. Meanwhile, Mr. Nayak called me into his office and I knew he would be asking about the 'Three-layered sandwich'.

Management Lessons from Cricket

"I want you to lead this transformational project", Mr. Nayak bowled a juicy half volley at me.

While I was just about to drive the loose ball to the boundary, something supernatural stopped me. It can't be that easy, it could be a googly.

"But I have no experience of leading big projects", I was a bit hesitant and wanted to see if the ball turns.

It actually did.

"I want a young person without the baggage of experience. The person leading this initiative would also ensure these baggage (stubborn) minds are aligned. You may encounter difference of opinions from your senior team members"

Hmm... *"Stubborn minds", "that's a bouncer, don't go for it"*, my inner voice stopped me.

"Sir, we have many experienced team members", I again tried to duck under the bouncer.

"I just hate this word, 'EXPERIENCE", the experience of hunting cannot make Cat, a Lion", replied Mr. Nayak in a commanding tone. He pushed me out of my comfort zone and wanted me to think like an entrepreneur.

Suddenly, I could feel an adrenaline rush throughout my body. I felt powerful and had a hard hit on the juicy half volley for a boundary and said, "Yes Sir, we will make it happen". I was more excited as it was a huge learning opportunity.

"I want a person with the right mix of **Attitude, Skills,** and **Knowledge**, and that's my three-layered sandwich", Mr. Nayak narrated this with a winning smile and a 30⁰ tilted face towards his right. Even today, I remember that winning smile with a tilted face as if he had shared the secret formula of "Invisibility" but it is no less powerful than that.

"Don't worry, I will guide you throughout. Further, if the project is successful, the credit will go to you but if it fails, responsibility is mine", Mr. Nayak gave a pat on my back while resonating these golden words. That was the most inspiring leadership style I had ever experienced.

"We need to form a core team of people with the right mix of Attitude, Skills, and Knowledge", Mr. Nayak started teaching me his famous or infamous three-layered sandwich.

A-S-K: The Three Layered Sandwich

He pulled a sheet of paper and drew a triangle with sides named, Attitude, Skill, and Knowledge.

1. **Attitude**
2. **Skill**
3. **Knowledge**

He believed that these three are the key ingredients for

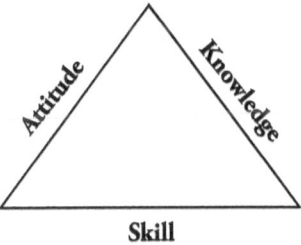

high performance. Improving skill and knowledge would develop expertise but this would only work in presence of a positive attitude. Hence, for any task to be successful, one needs to have:

a. **The right mix** of ASK to make a perfect triangle
b. **Willingness** to increase the area of the triangle. This can only be done by increasing the length of either or combination of sides. The length of the sides can be increased through learning, sharing, and execution.

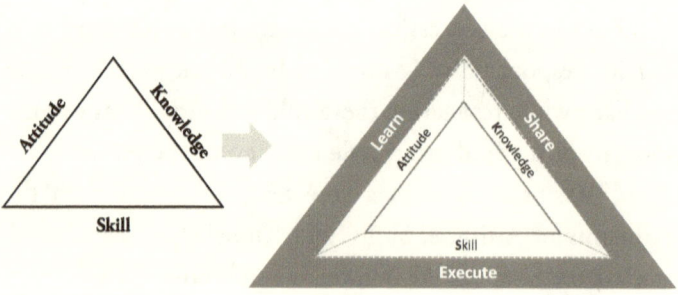

It is said that **Learning** improves Attitude, **Sharing** improves Knowledge and **Execution** improves Skill

Mr. Nayak wanted to select his core team based on the above approach. He wanted every person in the plant to be engaged in 5S while the core team would play the role of facilitators. It looked as if he was planning his moves like an experienced warrior.

I could easily relate the ASK concept in selecting the right partners during one of my **startups on digital learning**. I had selected a vendor for creating an e-learning website on Lean Manufacturing. Instead of using standard modules, the programmer wrote codes to enable customized learning based on the learning program selected by the customer. He had the right attitude and knowledge but was lacking skills. There was no need to re-invent the wheel when we could have used standard plug and play modules. It was my biggest mistake and after this experience, I always prefer ready-made solutions. At times, learning comes at a huge price.

ATM: Attitude Testing Mechanism

"Skill" and "Knowledge" develop expertise in a specific domain. While we could test a person on both of these by asking subject-related questions but how could Attitude be tested? Mr. Nayak had a simple 3 point mechanism to assess attitude. Every person makes mistakes but a person with a positive attitude would:

1. **A**ccept his mistakes
2. **T**ake Responsibility for his actions
3. **M**akes the best of them by learning

He would **never look for a hook** i.e. he would never look for a reason to hook his mistakes. So, if we ask a person about mistakes in his life then we could easily figure out his attitude from the details of his answer.

Finally, after meeting all team members, Mr. Nayak gave a rating to each member on the parameters of "Attitude", "Skill" and "Knowledge". He gave maximum weightage to "Attitude" as he believed being a positive-minded team player is the most important aspect. He also respected "expertise" but having a positive attitude was paramount. Simply putting, he was always looking out for **experts with the right attitude**.

He was very clear in creating a structure for high performance hence he outsourced 5S training to one of the reputed "experts" even though he was himself an excellent coach. Again he used his famous ASK technique to shortlist the agency. After every ingredient was in place, it was time to lit the fire. Finally, the kick-off date was announced to initiate the transformational project.

On the designated day, we all took our seats in the meeting room, and suddenly there was a pin drop silence when Mr. Nayak entered the room. He looked like a colonel marching with his firm, measured, and confident footsteps. After the formal welcome address, he asked the team about their understanding of 5S Implementation. As expected by now, everyone had googled 5S and were already Ph.D. holders in the subject. After hearing a couple of answers, Mr. Nayak was not amused and was quick to point out that, "I asked for 5S implementation"…he stressed "Implementation".

He then asked me, if I had any clue about the implementation. I said, "I could link 5S to my Engineering college hostel days in three steps".

Firstly, whenever I had to clean my study table drawer *(although it was a quarterly affair)*, I would first start with pulling out all the stuff from the drawer and then sort the stuff out that I did NOT need.

Secondly, I would then arrange the required stuff in the drawer in terms of frequency of usage i.e. putting the stationery in front and some key instruments and documents at the back of the drawer so that I save time in finding the items again.

Thirdly, after re-arranging, I would physically clean the place with a cloth and it looked shining clean at least for that day.

Before I could wind up my thoughts, Mr. Nayak exclaimed with joy, "The above three stages are the first three steps of 5S. It is more of a commonsense and we follow these steps day in and day out". Mr. Nayak showcased the positive change that the project would bring to all our lives. He then announced the core team and asked me to lead the project. He emphasized that the core team would only be a facilitator while everyone would play a key role in the project.

I had a core team that was highly energized along with a clear vision and a plan to transform. I could then feel the winds of change in the way, I see the world.

Entrepreneurship Takeaways

- This section gave important learning to select growth partners (employees, vendors, outsourced agencies, etc.).
- We should analyze people from:
  a. The **perspective of ASK**
  b. How keen they are to **increase the area** of their triangle
- Use **ATM** to gauge the attitude of people. Identify people with the right attitude. Negative people will always look for a hook.

- Being an expert is important but having a positive attitude is paramount. Hence focus on developing the expertise of the people who have the right attitude.
- In a start-up, one should always keep core competency in-house and outsource key activities to experts. Outsourcing key activities drive efficiencies and reduce the risk of high investments in setting up processes and resources.

3

What's in for Me (WIFM)

> *"When people are financially invested, they want a return. When people are emotionally invested, they want to contribute."*
>
> – Simon Sinek

Mr. Nayak was very particular in developing the skill level of the core team. He was a unique type of leader who taught us, **How Best Fails!!**

In the first place, we did not understand his objective. He then explained, "5S initiative would lead to many changes and the first obvious reaction of the people would be to resist the change, even before understanding it."

> *"If you want to make enemies, try to change something"*
>
> – Woodrow Wilson

Even the best fails by working in isolation
He further elaborated, "Even the best of organizations fail to execute projects effectively which looked simple on the drawing board. It is very crucial to connect early with key stakeholders to design & create their buy-in. The best case would be to create awareness amongst key stakeholders and get them engaged early."

The key to success is to create people's buy-in by connecting early and ensuring their engagement.
Mr. Nayak wanted the 5S initiative to go well beyond the office to touch everyone's personal life. Now, I can relate this with "Swachh Bharat Abhiyaan" *(Clean India Mission)*. It is 5S with a very high degree of people's engagement. The core of this initiative lies in creating awareness and engagement amongst the masses about cleanliness.

> *"There is no power for change greater than a community discovering what it cares about"*
>
> – Margaret J. Wheatley

Change is very sensitive as it affects people's emotions. Difference of opinion should always be respected and infact leveraged to bring out the best. We all were mesmerized by Mr. Nayak's clarity of thought and the way he was able to transfer his excitement to us. We learnt two ways of leveraging difference of opinion and creating People's Buy-in:

a. WIFM
b. Knoster Model

a. WIFM (What's In For Me)

We looked at difference of opinions from the stakeholder's perspective and answered **"What's in for me"** i.e. why stakeholders would support a change unless there is something beneficial for them.

We were able to strike a chord with all stakeholders through WIFM. The key lies in connecting early and let people discover what they care about. We linked the impact of 5S change to the WIFM. Example: We designed and communicated the following WIFM to support the 5S initiative:

5S success WIFM:

i. 5S Impact 1: Improve working conditions
WIFM 1: *Joy of working in a clean and safe workplace*

ii. 5S Impact 2: Ease out work pressures
WIFM 2: *Enjoy work & spend quality time with family*

iii. 5S Impact 3: Skill Enhancement
WIFM 3: *Learn new skills*

So, the stakeholders knew that there is something beneficial for them when they support a change. All employees were engaged and were sharing their suggestions even before the project had started. I learnt that most complex problems have simple solutions and simple solutions have higher acceptance and last longer. 5S is a really powerful tool and its essence lies in its simplicity. It had created positive vibes across the organization.

For an entrepreneurial mind, a crystal clear WIFM is very crucial, as it answers why the stakeholders will support the change. Why your team, investors, and customers will buy your idea i.e. everyone looks for *"What's in for me (WIFM)?"* Hence you need to design WIFM for all stakeholders for a win-win situation.

b. **Knoster Model**

Knoster model is a simple yet powerful tool that focuses on five key enablers for effective change i.e.

Vision, Skill, Incentives, Resources, and Action Plan

We referred to it by its acronym VSIRA *(pronounced as Vasira)*. We created a rule to answer the following questions before making any recommendations for a change:

Vision	Why are we proposing a change?
Skills	What skills are required for change?
Incentives	Why people will support change? It is **WIFM**
Resources	What resources are required? Do we have them in-house?
Action Plan	Have we created a detailed action plan? Are stakeholders aligned?

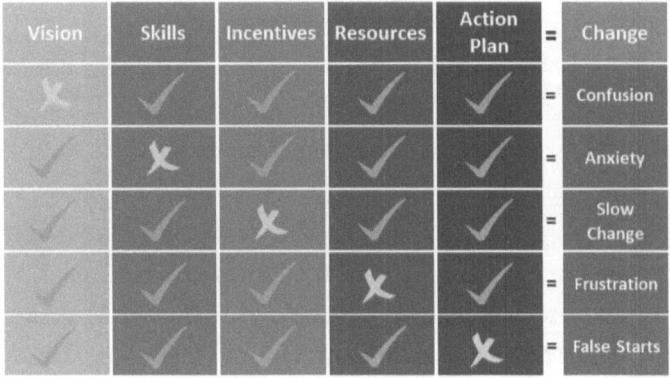

Fig: Knoster Model of Change Management

If any of the five ingredients are missing then change may not be effective. For example, refer figure above:

i. If "Vision" for change is missing and we have skills, Incentives, Resources, and an Action Plan then it would lead to **Confusion** as everyone would be disoriented about the outcome.
ii. Similarly, if "Skills" are missing then it would lead to **Anxiety** as the team would like to do work but lack essential skills. This would make them anxious.

We understood that just proposing a change and making its execution plan, would not make it successful. We designed **WIFM** to engage people and then used **VSIRA** for effective execution.

So, we were able to create positivity and buy-in amongst all employees to drive the 5S project. Mr. Nayak had given us the wings and the reason to fly, it was on us to show how well we could fly.

Entrepreneurship Takeaways

- An Entrepreneur may face resistance to his idea but he needs to **design WIFM**. The outcome from WIFM are the levers that an entrepreneur needs to use to engage people.
- A simple idea can also be an instant hit if it solves larger community problems through mass engagement.
- If there are multiple stakeholders then WIFM design needs to ensure a win-win situation. **Example: Fitness apps**. Subscribers download fitness app which:

    a. Helps them track their physical activities
    b. Creates engagement by enabling competition amongst friends
    c. Rewards them points for activities that can be monetized to buy merchandise from the app platform

    Hence it creates a win-win platform for app entrepreneurs, subscribers, and merchandise sellers

- After WIFM, one should focus on VSIRA. It will bring clarity before working out the finer implementation details. Hence the idea should pass the test of WIFM & VSIRA

4

5S: The Hidden Treasure

> *It is very important to know what to do,*
> *But more important to know what NOT to do,*
>
> – SMR

5S is a powerful tool and its essence lies in its simplicity. We attended training sessions and started with the first phase of 5S, i.e. "Sort".

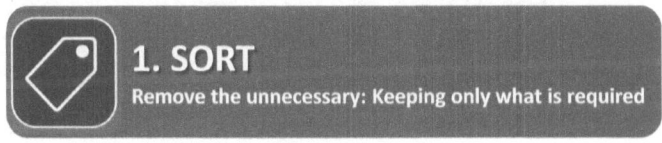

1. SORT
Remove the unnecessary: Keeping only what is required

Mantra #1: When in doubt, move it out

We clicked pictures of the area in the current situation which we would be comparing later with pictures of the sorted area. Sorting is an easy three-step technique:

1. Prepare a list of all items: Stationary, Tools, documents, etc.
2. Segregate listed items into **3** categories

Category	Items	Action
A	Required Items	Organize and keep
B	Not Required Items	Discard
C	Uncertain Items	Keep required, Discard rest

I thought there would be only two categories i.e. "Required" and "Not Required". Now, what is left? Is there any need for a third category? YES, we need this third category and in-fact this is the most important category.

Items which we don't know whether are required or not. We keep these items in case they are required in the future. These are called **Uncertain** Items.

3. Take action on each category
After sorting, we were surprised to see that uncertain items were maximum in numbers. It was easy to deal with category "A" items i.e. keep them in an organized manner. While Category "B" items were red-tagged and discarded.

But we had no plan for category "C" items and to deal with this, we kept them at a common area for everyone to see. We found few takers for some of these items and then we discarded the rest.

Sorting released a huge space and the area was then looking bigger, lighter, and ready for the next phase of transformation.

Funny Facts about category "C" items:

- No one knows where they are when needed
- Occupy more mental space than physical space
- The funniest part is that, we would be anyway discarding uncertain items after keeping them for years.

Identify and get rid of Uncertain items quickly else sooner we might need a new space to store them

On similar lines, an entrepreneur needs to create a framework within which his start-up will operate and must not dilute it unless fully tested. It is very important to sort-out what not to focus on i.e. as an entrepreneur you may need to outsource certain activities to experts and not try to be a jack of all trades. This clarity is crucial.

We extended 1S to our laptops too. This exercise was even tougher than physical sorting. After Sorting, we were left with only Category A items. These were hidden treasures.

Eventually, we were able to look beyond 5S i.e. from physical to cerebral 5S that helped in shaping the mind for entrepreneurship. We could feel the power of sorting, as it had even started impacting our minds too. Our mind continuously generates a lot of thoughts, ideas, and options. Hence we need to have a laser-sharp focus on the objective while evaluating options.

2. SET IN ORDER
A place for everything and everything in its place:
Fixed locations and clear visualisations

Mantra #2: A place for everything and everything in its place

The objective for the team was very clear:

"No one would waste time searching for an item"

We explored best practices of Visual Management to store and locate an item.

All "Required" items should have a designated storage location. High usage items were placed on innovative shadow boards as depicted in the picture. Just at the glimpse of the shadow board, we could make out the missing piece and the same was restored quickly.

From nuts and bolts to engines, from raw material to finished goods, we designed innovative storage concepts.

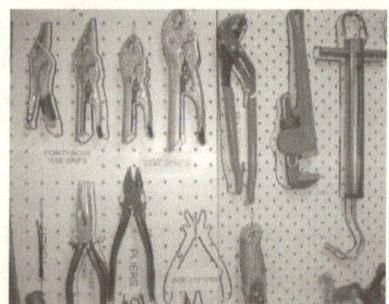

This activity showcased the creative side of people. The team was receptive to new ideas and concepts. Visual Management had put storage on Auto-pilot mode. It improved productivity as no one was wasting time looking for an item.

Linking this aspect to start-ups, "A place for everything and everything in its place" is the first step for putting operations on Autopilot mode. Further, most of the entrepreneurs are creative and leverage visual management to make customer connect platforms like websites, landing pages, and even physical site visits very effective. **An idea presented using symbols, colours and flow charts connects instantly**.

A Unique Interview: Do It-Get It

We felt the need for a purchase professional who could understand different storage concepts and get them procured. I interviewed a few purchase engineers and shortlisted three of them. Mr. Nayak called them one by one to his cabin and there was a surprise waiting for them.

He gave the same component to each of them individually. The ask was to source the component i.e., to find the supplier and cost of the component in one hour. I found it to be a very unique style of gauging efficiency rather than formal interaction.

The first engineer, who was exceptionally good in his communication skills, came back in an hour saying that he had discussed with 3 different suppliers and the component can only be sourced from New Delhi. He seemed very confident to identify the supplier and the cost in the next 2 days.

The second engineer, who was interacting just to the point, told us that the component was available in the

Bhagirath place market in New Delhi. The market was closed that day and hence the price can be ascertained only the next day. He was quite impressive.

Finally, the third engineer came back asking us the number of components to be ordered. He had found the supplier and was already negotiating. The more components we order, the better the cost we could get. We asked him about his process to connect with the supplier. He shared that he could locate the component in the Bhagirath place market in New Delhi but the market was closed. Then he figured out the email details of three suppliers through a search engine and mailed them about an excellent opportunity to supply in a multinational company. Interestingly, a couple of them reverted him immediately and he was already negotiating.

Mr. Nayak was quick to select the third engineer as he could find the right mix of ASK. That day, I had practically seen the importance of ASK *(our three-layered sandwich)*

> *"What we believe in, we can see it"*
>
> – SMR

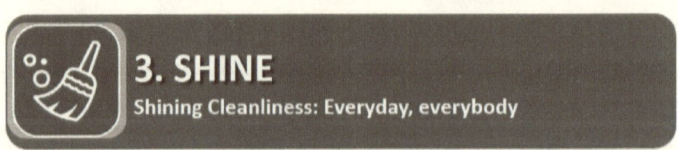

Mantra #3: Shining Cleanliness

Cleanliness is everyone's responsibility and not one person's job. We made an SOP (Standard Operating Procedure) to clean up one's area at the start of the day, may it be computers or machines.

This one was difficult to explain to some stubborn minds and we had a hard time to crack this. This was a huge change management issue as it was not acceptable to few colleagues to clean up their mess and they believed that it was merely a housekeeper's job.

> No one notices when you do it, but everyone notices it when you don't!!

Change Starts from Top

I recalled my last company, which was a white goods multinational company. The Managing Director of the company used to visit shop-floor with a mopping cloth and would start cleaning conveyor and other equipment. Then all personnel irrespective of their ranks were quick to follow him. MD visit always used to be a surprise but was very frequent. Soon it became an organization-wide movement as it was driven from the top. This activity motivated line managers to clean up their workplaces daily and they considered it as part of their job and felt pride in it. It then became a habit and then part of their culture.

I tried the same trick here and took the help of Mr. Nayak to make it an organization-wide movement. He welcomed the step and was happy to do it but in his style. He planned surprise visits to shop floors with a mopping cloth and would start cleaning equipment and the whole team would follow him. The only difference was that he would then share the importance of cleanliness and linked it to safety. He played the WIFM as "Safety" and made it a mass engagement.

The trick worked, worked again… "

> *Cultural change flows from Top to Bottom.*
> *Practicing a concept daily makes it a habit,*
> *And then it becomes a culture*
>
> **– SMR**

Cleanliness is a very big topic of discussion in India. We are now progressing towards "Swachh Bharat" (Clean India) and witnessing a positive change in the way people treat and interact with their surroundings and environment. Everyone has a responsibility and should do his bit. Truly, one can be a torchbearer but change happens only through mass engagement.

It is said that the battle is won if we implement the first 3S religiously.

We were just 2 months into the project and things had started getting challenging with inter-departmental issues and conflicts pertaining to change management. Mr. Nayak was quick to sense the pulse and he decided to recharge the team. He wanted us to break out from monotony and be more adventurous and think out of the box solutions.

We planned an offsite to celebrate the success of the first 3S. It was planned in a huge sprawling lush green resort at the outskirts of the city. The day was planned in small sessions and it ended with a special surprise for all of us. It was a cricket match under the floodlights. Almost every Indian gets excited by the idea of cricket. We all are like born cricketers, it flows in our veins. We live and breathe Cricket, it **unites** us. Although most of us had not played for ages, but everyone was in for it. It was an amazing experience to play under the lights with professional infrastructure.

The weather too was adorable with the sun setting down leaving the sky with a picture-perfect shot of red, amber, and wine colors, hinting at *good times* ahead. Actually, beauty lies in the eyes of the beer holder.

Drinks were served during the match at the makeshift pavilion. Players were seen frequently crossing the boundary for spirits. High spirits had eventually turned fast bowlers to spinners and spinners to spectators. The objective of the match was very clear and we attained it in a very entertaining way. It united us as one team focused on a mission.

> ***Adventure may hurt, but monotony will kill.***
>
> **– Anonymous**

4. STANDARDISE
Same standard, everytime for everybody:
Do the right things, the right way, everytime

STANDARDIZATION IS ...

THE CONSISTENCY OF THE WORK SEQUENCE.

Mantra #4: Do the right things, the right way, every time

In the first 3S, we observed that one function was much more focused on 1S (Sort) while the other was more inclined towards 3S (Shine). This was primarily due to the nature of work and the working styles of people.

Every team was working in their way and we felt a very strong need of binding all the loose ends together by developing a standard system that would be common for all.

> *"Systems Work, People Network."*
>
> – SMR

Mr. Nayak believed that stringent systems kill creativeness and make people slaves of the system itself. Systems are like rubber-band, they help keep things together but at the same time, too many rubber-bands create stress. Systems are developed to get consistent results while people are to be leveraged to network, innovate, execute and lead.

We developed simple guidelines for implementing the first 3S through Visual Display boards. The 4thS is very crucial as it ensures the consistency of outcomes. It enables a sense of oneness like we have standard school uniforms, standard protocols in the army.

Entrepreneurs should focus on creating digital systems to automate transactional work requiring a high degree of repeatability and consistency. Systems are the backbone to achieve Consistency.

5. SUSTAIN
Maintain Discipline: Sustaining the habit

Mantra #5: Review to Sustain & Continue

Sustenance of initiatives is the key to ensure continuity. The objective was to make it a habit and this was achieved through:

- Periodic Review
- Reward and Recognition
- Training and Communication

Review is a mechanism for self-reflection that helps in timely course corrections. There was a fear across team members by the name "review". We found a one-word answer to integrate 5S into the system, motivate stakeholders, and create a sense of achievement.

We created competition across functions and named it "**5S Winning Shot**" to give a more positive message.

Finally, the most important aspect was Rewards and Recognition. It is said that leaders praise in public and criticize in private. We celebrated winners as "Champions" with appreciation letters and trophies.

Driving Out Fear Improves Engagement

The most important change was in the attitude of the team. They were change agents at office, home, and in their communities. The exciting journey that started with workplace organization finally lead to the transformation of minds.

An orderly desk and clarity of thoughts are a reflection of an organized mind.

It was 7:00 pm at a posh hotel in Faridabad and all of us shouted with joy, "three cheers" on our 5S success. It was a memorable 8 months journey and we recalled:

The moments of agony, conflicts, and fights,
Hard decisions, when things went left and right,
Finally the moments of victory and pride.

Entrepreneurship Takeaways

1S
- Our mind is an Engine of Ideas. It is very important to know what TO DO but more important to figure out **what NOT TO DO**

- It is always better to be known as an expert in one area rather than a jack of all i.e. **identify one's micro-niche**. For Example:

    a. Mathematics teacher vis-à-vis all subject teacher
    b. Weight loss dieticians are high in demand over general dieticians as they have a specific niche

2S

- Visual management can make customer connect platforms like websites, landing pages, and even physical site visits very effective. **An idea presented using symbols, colours and flow charts connects instantly**
- "**A place for everything and everything in its place**" is the first step to put operations on Auto-pilot mode
- Judging people's effectiveness from the perspective of **ASK is far better than a formal interaction**

3S

- Cleanliness directly flows from physical space to our minds and eventually gets reflected in our work. It unclutters our minds for innovative ideas

4S

- **Systems Work, People Network:** Systems are the backbone for consistent customer experience
- Entrepreneurs should focus on **creating systems** to make things simple and fast for customers by putting repeatable tasks on autopilot mode

5S

- Entrepreneurship is a journey where one needs to make several course corrections hence **self-reflection and a coach review is a critical element**
- An orderly desk and clarity of thoughts are a reflection of an organized mind

PHASE 2

The Transformation

5

Corporate Junction

> *A bend in the road is not the end of the road unless you fail to make the turn.*
>
> – Helen Keller

A call from the world's largest consulting firm "Deloitte", catapulted my career. It was for their "Strategy and Operations" (S&O) vertical and I did not know about these fancy terms then. My new boss, Gaurav, who was a Partner of the S&O vertical, was a real champ in communication and was always spot on in conveying his ideas.

It was an astronomical transition for me, from being interacting with the manufacturing team to a corporate team. It meant a shift from:

- Calling your boss as "Sir" to first name
- Office uniform to business suits
- Shop floor to a modern office with lavish workspaces
- Discussing production numbers to corporate discussions ranging from Businesses, Strategies, Economy, Thought Leadership, Case Studies, etc

It was a different world altogether. Initially, I kept aloof until I made some real friends who made me homogenous quite fast.

Being a Consultant

Although sarcastic, being a consultant does not empowers one to keep poking its nose on every dish, to advise on the recipe. There is one thing that is readily available at every nook and corner i.e. advice. The beauty of this role is to charge for a service that is perceived as free. Here, one needs to be "*Jack of all but master of one*".

Initially, I got trained on sharpening communication skills, key tools & techniques, and global best practices. There is a unique advantage of working in a consulting organization that it leads to an overall development which is a blend of:

- Technical skills........................*Domain knowledge*
- Entrepreneurial skills ....*Solution-focused*
- Leadership skills...............*Business communication*
- Project Management skills ....*Project execution*
- Networking Skills ....*Customer engagement*

The most important aspect was networking. The best way to learn is to apply concepts practically rather than in a classroom.

> *The richest people in the world look for and build networks; everyone else looks for work*
>
> **– Robert Kiyosaki**

Engagement: The Core of Networking

I accompanied Gaurav (Partner) for my first client meeting at Noida. The client was a well-known brand in the Food & Beverage segment in North India.

Gaurav initiated the discussion informally with politics, then transitioned to the Football world cup, then to the predictions of "Paul" the Octopus, in the Football world cup of 2010. It was all seamless and perfect.

I was amazed to see how quickly Gaurav was able to link football matches with higher sales in restaurants and bars that excited the potential client. He was able to establish an emotive connect and the client was then more open in sharing his challenges and expectations. We further leveraged the platform created by Gaurav and shared Industry challenges and potential solutions along with best practices.

We focused on F&B lean practices, quicker delivery mechanisms, logistics solutions for multi-location food chains, food wastages, raw material variances, etc.

We eventually won the project in the next couple of meetings but for me, we had won it in the first meeting itself.

3 Winning Secrets for a Successful Meeting Outcome

1. Design CST (Core objective, Strategy, Tactics)

Understand the core objective of the meeting and develop a strategy to meet the objective. For example, the core objective of the meeting was to showcase that we understand the pain points and have a solution for the same. We designed our strategy to focus on the value to address the specific needs of the customer. Rest everything we did, to achieve the strategy was mere tactics.

Tactics are the actions that we take to achieve a broader strategy. The higher the clarity on strategy, the higher the chances of designing effective tactics.

> ***Strategy without tactics is the slowest route to victory.***
> ***Tactics without strategy is the noise before defeat.***
>
> **– Sun Tzu**

2. Preempt the flow

Preempt the meeting flow based on the agenda of stakeholders before the interaction. Preparation before a meeting is more important than the meeting itself.

For example, we prepared well before the meeting on 5 key aspects (**CLOVE**):

- **Challenges**: Understanding of Industry & client business and challenges
- **Low hanging fruits:** Potential solutions to challenges along with low hanging fruits for an immediate benefit
- **Offer:** An irresistible offer
- **Value**: How can we add real value to get the client excited i.e. the differentiator
- **Experience**: Experience of similar projects

We wanted the meeting to remain focused on the above aspects, hence we had a clear path before the meeting to steer it for a designed outcome.

> *Victorious warriors win first and then go to war, while defeated warriors go to war first and then seek to win*
>
> – Sun Tzu

3. Networking

Networking is not just limited to having a large number of contacts in the list. It means the way we:

- Connect
- Establish a bond of trust
- Create an environment of sharing to create higher value for the customer

The first impression is very crucial and long-lasting. To break the ice, one needs to communicate with the customer on his area of interest. Then leverage and link the area of interest to drive the objective, keeping customer value at the core. Hence one needs to be updated in multi-dimensions, especially in sports, geopolitical scenarios, customer behavior, etc. to kick start the discussion.

The objective should be to take the discussion to higher engagement levels by sharing relevant information that excites customers like **low-hanging fruits, best practices**, etc. Sharing of content is crucial but engagement is paramount.

> *Content is King but*
> *engagement is Queen and the lady rules the house!*
>
> — **Mari Smith**

Entrepreneurship Takeaways

- Draw out strategy from the broader objective and tactics from the strategy
- While developing strategy and tactics, the focus should remain on **creating real value for the customer**
- Preempt and design the meeting flow. Use **CLOVE** to prepare well for key meetings to achieve designed outcomes
- Product is king but engagement is queen, and the lady rules the house. **Entrepreneurs should focus on connecting and engaging with targeted customers**

6

The Master Stroke

> *"Get closer than ever to your customers.
> So close that you tell them what they need
> well before they realize it themselves."*
>
> – Steve Jobs

The Masterstroke dwells on the power of customer experience to drive exponential growth. I am sharing a transformational project and the way we lead it for  astronomical growth for us and customer. This project sowed the seeds of starting small and scaling up while keeping customer value at the core.

A Transformational Project

An automotive component manufacturer based in Gurgaon called us for a diagnostic study of their plant. They wanted to revive their profit margins. We studied their operations for 2 days, interviewed key personnel, and collected relevant data. We then drew value stream maps, focused on precise measuring of bottleneck processes, analyzed the data, and developed recommendations. It is an awesome proverb, **"Measure is Treasure"** and we were going to experience the power of this proverb.

Baseline Facts

The company was manufacturing 54 different types of components. They were operating for 24 hours (2 shifts of 12 hours each) in a day with almost nil profit margins. The margins had depleted over a period of time due to increasing costs and price reduction targets by OEMs. Managers & supervisors were always on a fire fighting mode to ensure timely supplies to OEMs. We focused our study only on 6 out of 54 components which accounted for 80% of their revenues.

Key Findings

Precise measuring and analysis of bottleneck processes made us recommend that the whole operation could ideally be done in 16 hours. The Managing Director (MD) of the company wanted to understand the recommendations. I and Gaurav went to meet him who introduced us to his Vice President, Mr. Ghosh. He was a short man wearing thick spectacles with a heavy voice depicting a typical Bengali ascent. He looked very skeptical about the project from the first meeting itself.

We shared our analysis with them and proposed that their company worked for 24 hours a day while the same work could be done in 16 hours. There were some inefficiencies in the system and we could do the project for them in 4 months.

Winning a Project is the Start of An Experience

We followed our tried and tested CLOVE technique and show-cased low-hanging fruits which could be implemented quickly. Mr. Ghosh was obviously not amused and argued that inefficiencies would always be there. Further, he yelled that it was not possible to make it 16 hours as he had set up the plant and had an experience of 30 years.

MD was very composed and at the same time very positive as he wanted this to happen. He calmed Mr. Ghosh and persuaded him to let us try and in-fact asked him to lead the project. It was like keeping a cat to guard the milk.

We showcased our credentials to build confidence and proposed linking 80% of our fees to the desired outcome to make it an irresistible offer. MD also assured us of a new project at his new plant which was under construction nearby, if we successfully delivered the project.

Kick It Off

The project was started with great zeal with a kick-off meeting with Mr. Ghosh, Plant supervisors, and our 3 member team. We prioritized the improvement opportunities and the biggest one was re-layouting of 40 machines on the shop floor to avoid zig-zag movement. Each operator used to walk approx. 4 miles in a day taking material from one process to another. With re-layouting, this distance was going to reduce to just 0.6 miles.

Twist in the Game

We were a week into the project and started getting resistance from the workforce and its magnitude kept on increasing day by day. We were using communication mechanisms for change management but nothing seemed to work. Then we met supervisors to understand the real core issue. Each operator used to get paid for 8 hours of standard work plus 4 hours of overtime as the plant run for 2 shits of 12 hours each. But the outcome from our project would mean that the plant would run only for 16 hours, that is, 2 shifts of 8 hours each and then no one would earn overtime. Hence, the operators were not supporting it.

Pack-Up

Meanwhile, during the meeting, I got a call from Mr. Ghosh to meet him immediately. I went to his office and he seemed like a victorious man with a cunning smile. He told me to stop the project as it would lead to a major IR (Industrial Relations) issue and the last thing he could imagine was people protesting at the gate of the company. He was in such a hurry to announce his victory that he didn't even want to spend a minute talking to me and called up Gaurav to abandon the project. Before I could realize it, the project was called off.

It was a huge setback for me professionally and I could not sleep that night. I kept on thinking about the sequence of events starting from the diagnostic study. How could I miss such a vital piece of information that every operator would lose because of this project?

But also, how long the business could survive with nil margins?

I realized that we were only concentrating on technical aspects to turn it around while the WIFM aspect was completely missed.

Back with a Bang

I checked the watch, it was 4:00 am and I went for a walk. During the walk, suddenly one thing hit my mind like a flash. I remembered the company's MD saying that he was building a new plant and if that was true then he would need manpower to run that plant. Now, If I could rework my whole plan again from 16 hours working to 12 hours then every person would get 4 hours overtime and the extra workforce who used to do second shift could be transferred to the new plant.

I quickly went back home and reworked the value stream map to bring down the working hours from 16 to 12. I figured out that we could do this by focusing on 5 aspects:

a. Re-layouting 50 machines instead of 40
b. Investing in 3 machines (2 welding and 1 drilling jigs)
c. Investing in pick and move trolleys
d. Reducing the rejection rate
e. Moving 20% of the operators from 2nd to 1st shift

These could bring down the working time to 12 hours with 75% efficiency. I was feeling very confident and was waiting to discuss this with Gaurav at the office. He was also very supportive and took no time in understanding and valuing this option. He immediately called upon the company's MD to discuss this proposal further.

We were back in the board room with the MD and Mr. Ghosh. It was not easy to convince them as it involved some investments but the return on investment was just 3 months hence it was too lucrative for them to reject.

Fastened Seat Belts, Sleeves Rolled Up for a Comeback

The next day afternoon, we were back in the company with heads high up in confidence to revive the project. The first thing we did was to connect with Mr. Ghosh and then with supervisors to share the benefits of the revised project deliverables.

It looked like Mr. Ghosh was in love with inefficiencies and had a blind trust that these would not leave the system rather we would leave again. This time we were extra cautious with WIFM and ensured every activity was led by a supervisor with our team backing them with calculations.

It took us 4 months to complete the project. Eventually, what looked like an impossible task, we made it happen. The plant transitioned from 24 hours to 12 hours even with 15% increased demand from OEM. 20% of the people who were in the 2nd shift were moved to the first shift while the rest of the people were transferred to the new plant.

The project that was called off, got revived again by converting risk into an opportunity for all stakeholders.

- Operators were happy and supported new processes as their physical efforts had reduced due to less movement and their financial benefit had actually increased
- Managers and supervisors had started enjoying a great work-life balance
- The financial benefits achieved for the company were twice than committed hence we earned a handsome variable fee

Although Mr. Ghosh was skeptical about the improvements and challenged us on many occasions during the project but that helped us prepare well.

> *A good opponent makes you a better player*
>
> *– SMR*

The Real Game: The Master Stroke

The customer was already excited by the gains achieved and with the speed of project execution. The value that we created was evident. Hence, we were awarded 4 new projects for their other 3 plants. The success of this project opened gates to other auto-component manufacturers. This became a huge global case study in all our client meetings. In addition to winning new projects through their references, we were being traced by manufacturing companies for Lean Manufacturing projects.

We leveraged the success of this project horizontally and vertically i.e.:

- Winning new engagements with the same client
- Leveraging references of the client
- Leveraging it as a case study for new companies and industries
- Adding more value by expanding Lean Manufacturing to Lean Six Sigma

The essence of the masterstroke lies in creating huge value for the customer which could be further leveraged for new business opportunities. While we explore new business opportunities the focus should remain on creating sustained customer value. Some may call it up-selling but it only works if you have delighted your customer in the first service.

Entrepreneurship Takeaways

- It is paramount to deliver value to the customer and the customer should feel it.
- While delivered value is leveraged for upselling opportunities, the focus should be again on creating more value for the customer. Hence the concept of

starting small and scaling up has **sustained customer value** always at the core.

- An entrepreneur could work on upselling strategy, as:

    a. **Base Product**: Highest selling product, easy for the target customer to buy and he sees a real value in it. This is the most economical offering

    b. **Core Product**: This is the mainstay product and is priced higher than the base product. It can either be a standalone offering or customers who buy the base product can get graduated to this

    c. **High Premium Product**: This is a top-notch product. An entrepreneur should graduate its customers to the next higher level to increase the value delivered and ensure higher revenues

7

Out of the Box Thinking

*Innovative Ideas take birth when there is no BOX,
First, remove the box then start with the end in mind*

– SMR

What is a Box?

Box simply means limiting conditions. These are the boundaries within which one naturally thinks and takes decisions.

Example: A Frog in a well perceives it as an ocean and cannot even imagine any bigger

source of water than well. If I say to a person that he has two options then he will focus on choosing between the two and at best will try to optimize one of the options.

How Can One Think "Out of the Box"?

Broadly, it is a simple four-step technique. Again I do not wish to bind you in 4 steps ☺

1. Start with the end in mind
Be very clear about the final objective to be achieved. In the case of multiple objectives, prioritize and choose one. Example: A CEO wants to increase revenue and profitability from a product A

2. List all critical success factors (CSF) and inter-linkages
Write down all factors and sub-factors. Example: To improve profit from product A, you may wish to optimize CSF like Price, Cost, Sales volume, etc. Further, these will also have interlinkages with each other. Example: If we increase the price, sales volume may go down. If we increase features in a product then it may lead to cost increase etc.

3. **Simulate all possible decision options** based on CSF and interlinkages.

4. **Create an opportunity** for the best-case scenario. The same is explained below in an example.

A True "Out of the ~~BOX~~ Bucket" Case

I was once asked the following question by an Automobile company CFO. If we have to increase revenue and profitability, from the sale of grease buckets that are sold to dealers and then from dealers to final customers, then should we:

a. Increase its price and increase the profit per bucket but the sale volume will go down due to higher price, or
b. Decrease its price to ensure higher sales volume but this will reduce profit per bucket

Almost everyone in the client team preferred to increase prices in a phased manner to gauge the market. Can you guess, what we did? Basically, the two given options i.e. increase or decrease price is a BOX and we need to think beyond these two options.

The best-case scenario would be to increase both, revenue and profitability. We created a new opportunity for the best-case scenario.

The size of the grease bucket was 5 kg. After usage pattern analysis, we proposed a smaller 500 grams grease pouches with a nozzle. The pouch had to be squeezed for the grease to come out of the nozzle. So in addition to the existing 5 Kg grease bucket @ 750 bucks, we launched a 500 gm pouch @ 100 bucks. Earlier we could only sell an average of 100 buckets per day which meant Rs. 75 K as revenue per day.

In a couple of months, we could sell 1000 pouches and 70 buckets per day. The nozzle of the pouch helped in greasing hard-to-reach areas as well. This had doubled our revenue per day to 150 K. Further profitability of pouch was a lot higher than bucket hence it was a win-win situation for all stakeholders, as:

Customer: The higher value being created with ease of use due to nozzle, pocket-friendly product size
Dealer: Higher revenue and hence higher commission
OEM: Higher revenue and profitability
Scale-up Opportunity: Related Industries, Competition customers had also started buying the same.

> *Do not go where the path may lead, go instead where this no path and leave a trail."*
>
> – Ralph Waldo Emerson

The Pebbles of Wisdom: A Story Can Change Perspective

I could recall a childhood story shared by my father about the wisdom of a young girl. Once upon a time, there was a poor farmer who used to live with his daughter in a village that was surrounded by hills. He owed a huge loan to the village head which kept on increasing year after year even after paying him regularly. The village head was a crooked moneylender who used to trap villagers by lending them money at exorbitant interest rates.

The village head had evil intentions to marry farmer's beautiful daughter and was always thinking of ways and means to exploit his miserable situation. On one fine day, the village head called the farmer and proposed him a plan to get rid of his loan. The plan was to play a game, a game of luck, a game that could turn fortunes. The game was that the whole village would assemble at the base of the hill which had plenty of white and black pebbles. A person would pick a black and a white pebble and put them in a steel jar and cover it. Then the daughter of the farmer would pull out one pebble from the jar without looking inside it. If the pebble turns out to be white then all his loan would be forgiven and he could enjoy the rest of his life but if his daughter pulls out a black pebble then she would have to marry the village head and yet again his loan would be waived off. The poor farmer was confused as in either of the cases his loan would be waived off but he had a 50% risk of getting his daughter married to a crooked man.

The farmer came home and shared the game with his daughter. She understood the village head's plan to marry her. She wanted to help her father and yet did not want to marry the evil person. She insisted her father to play the game. On the selected day, the whole village gathered at the hill base. A stranger, who was hand in gloves with the village head, was chosen to pick one each of white and black pebbles. He smartly picked two black pebbles and quickly put them in the jar and covered it. The girl who was very alert as it was a game of life for her, noticed his mischievous act. The jar was then covered and given to the girl.

What Options She Had?

She was horrified at what she saw but kept her calm and thought of the options she had:

1. She could pull out a pebble which would obviously be black. She would then have to marry that crooked man who would ruin her life but the loan would be forgiven

2. Else, she could shout and let everyone know that both pebbles were black. This could again lead to any of the two scenarios:

    a. This act might make the village head angry and he would start screaming, putting the blame back on the girl and the game might be called off

    b. Or, this act might also lead to stranger admitting his mistake and the game might start all over again. This would again enable her a 50% chance of winning

She then thought of the best scenario that she wants.

What is the Best-Case Scenario?

The best case would be that she escapes the marriage and also gets the loan nullified. Neither of the above options could lead to the best scenario.

How the Best-Case Scenario is Possible?

She then thought if she could manage a white pebble from the jar, only then the best-case scenario could happen.

How can she CREATE an opportunity for the best case?

Then what happened next in the story, gives me goosebumps to date. She put her hand in the jar, pulled out a pebble, and dropped it hurriedly on earth in a way that it seemed like a slip. The earth was already covered with black and white pebbles so no one could figure out which one she picked. The village head shouted at her that how could the colour of the pebble be known? She apologized for the slip and softly replied that the colour of the pebble in the jar could help. If there was a black pebble in the jar then she would have pulled out a white one and vice versa.

The village head knew that there was a black pebble in the jar and the intelligent young girl had won the game. The options that the girl was thinking of earlier, was actually the box. Hence the focus should be on creating opportunities that lead us to the best-case scenario.

This is an inspiring story on out-of-the-box thinking which teaches us to create opportunities to meet the desired outcome. This was made possible by thinking with a broader perspective and leveraging the resources and situation in hand to covert risk into an opportunity.

> *"Great creators don't necessarily have the deepest expertise but rather seek out the broadest perspectives."*
>
> – Adam Grant

Entrepreneurship Takeaways

- Out of the box thinking and doing is the very genesis of being an Entrepreneur. Opportunities are created by thinking Out of the Box. **Entrepreneurs don't wait for an opportunity, they create it.**
- Thinking with a broader perspective and leveraging the resources and situation at hand can covert risk into an opportunity.
- Never let any condition put you inside a box. If you are non-decisive; try to see the Box, Just remove it.
- "Begin with the end in mind" is the most powerful way to get the thinking engine on the right track
- Always write down "Critical success factors", as we are too engrossed in transactional details so we tend to miss either CSFs or their linkages

PHASE 3

Business Modelling

8

The Front Force

Cracking the business model puzzle can be very tricky. In consulting, we engaged with prominent industry leaders and entrepreneurs to design and execute business models. I used business model canvas which was designed by Alex Osterwalder, and customized it to help businesses to design and analyze their business models.

I learnt that designing a winning business model boils down to three factors i.e. front force, value proposition, and the thrust engine. These three are the magical pillars and are detailed in the next three chapters. Front force leverages value proposition to acquire, retain and grow customers while Thrust Engine creates value proposition.

Front force means customer engaging activities which can be categorized as:

1. Fish the Niche
2. United Vision

3. Smart Channels
4. Insightful Relationships

| **Fish the Niche** | United Vision | Smart Channels | Insightful Relationships |

1. Fish the Niche

Gardening at rooftop
Kitchen gardening (KG) at rooftop
KG with drip irrigation (DI) at rooftop
KG with DI at rooftop in New Delhi

Niche product: KG with DI at rooftop
Niche market : New Delhi / Bungalows / Age: 50-60

Niche means a specific product or service for a targeted market segment. The product is not meant for mass consumption and it either kills pain or creates gain for a targeted segment. As depicted in the image above, an entrepreneur wants to explore business opportunities in the domain of gardening. He nails down the niche to Kitchen gardening with drip irrigation at the rooftop, for the customer segments based at New Delhi with bungalows. As a next step, a pilot test may be conducted for specific plants on a smaller customer base, say at South Delhi.

The key point is that you need to be very specific and be recognized as an expert in your respective niche. Do not try to sell to everyone rather focus your efforts on your specific target segment which will yield high conversion and lower acquisition cost.

"Fishing the niche" is the most crucial activity for an entrepreneur and the same is illustrated in 4 sections as:

   a. Test fast, fail fast, adjust fast
   b. 3 challenges in picking a niche and mitigating them
   c. 3 Rules of Niche market
   d. An effective way to identify Niche

a. Test fast, fail fast, adjust fast

Entrepreneurs look for their passion and try to evolve it as their niche. It is very important to come up with the right niche and test it. I recall way back in 2007, I started thinking about my passion for being a transformational coach. It took me 1 year to zero-in on my niche i.e. "Lean Six Sigma" training. Then I invested another two years in preparing the content and the online platform for delivering the modules. By then, I was already into analysis-paralysis mode and wanted my content to be the best in the world. I wanted to give an entirely fascinating learning experience to my audience. Finally, everything was ready by 2010 and I launched it for engineering students. My niche was Lean Six Sigma training and the niche market was engineering students in final year. After another 1 year of conducting demo sessions, I ended up realizing that it was a product-market misfit and even the delivery platform was not correct. The platform was a bit ahead of its time as mobile internet was not cost-effective in 2010. By then, I was at the point of no return due to a high degree of customization. Hence, it is utmost important to **test your niche fast for a small group,** refine it and if you fail, fail fast and learn fast.

> *Test fast, fail fast, adjust fast*
>
> – Tom Peters

b. 3 challenges in picking a niche and mitigating them
I wanted to be perfect and did not want to pick a wrong niche. This was the biggest mistake that I did in the early stages i.e. invested too much time in selecting the niche and more importantly, I tested the niche once the product was completely designed. I have categorized challenges and their solutions for picking niches under 3 categories:

- **There is nothing called a perfect niche**
  Budding entrepreneurs have been spending enormous time and efforts to identify their niche as they want it to be perfect. They have been poured on with the concept that they need to find what they love to do and everything else will fall in place. They want to zero-in on that perfect niche which would then become the purpose of their lives. They are obsessed with finding a niche that matches their DNA. People are always scared of picking a wrong niche and getting committed to it. But that's the beauty of the journey called entrepreneurship.

Being a perfectionist is the biggest obstacle to a startup. Hey, you are not finding your life partner and by the way, how many of us get the perfect partner, we all know. In section d "An effective way to identify niche", I will share a simple technique to pick your niche.

- **Do not get married to a niche**

    As time changes, markets change, choices and priorities of customers change, and hence there is nothing called a niche for life. It keeps on changing to address the changing market conditions. It is completely OK to change the niche but more important is to start working on a niche rather than looking for a niche for life. You are anyway not getting married to your niche, it is OK to move on. The idea should be to get committed to a niche, put everything behind it, test it on a smaller market, refine it, if you fail, fail fast, and learn fast.

- **Warriors are tested in war, not in the lab**

    It always payoff to seed and test your idea with the smaller but real customers even before you get your final product in shape. You can never expect an honest review from your family and friends. The reviewer has to always be a third person, ideally a real customer who critically evaluates your product.

> *"Everybody has a plan until they get punched in the face"*
>
> – Mike Tyson

Be ready to accept real honest reviews. It helps to refine the product by better understanding the expectations of the target market.

Secondly, the idea should be to "**Test it now**" rather than will do it once it is completely ready. It is always OK to fail in the test but it is always better to fail fast. That's the whole objective of the test, that it shows you the mirror and prepares you for the final bout. The test needs to be done like a litmus test which yields faster results. Hence one needs to start nimble and refine it as it goes on.

c. 3 Rules of Niche market

Like an entrepreneur works on a niche product, similarly niche market needs laser-sharp focus. If you are targeting everybody, you are targeting nobody. 3 Simple rules for identifying niche market are:

- Explore the ideal market for which your niche product will kill pain or create gain
- Explore if there is there any untapped micro market
- Narrow down the niche market in terms of

    - **Demographics** (how the customer looks): Age, Income, Family, Gender, Locality, Education, etc
    - **Psychographic** (how the customer thinks): Punctual, Serious, Intellect, Playful, Simple, Elegant, Vocal, etc
    - **Behavior** (how the customer behaves): Tech-savvy, Foodie, Traveler, Health freak, Sports enthusiast, etc

Better the streamlining, better the brand positioning, and more precise the targeting.

> ***Commit to a niche; try to stop being everything to everyone.***
>
> **– Andrew Davis**

d. An effective way to identify a Niche:

We have enabled people to identify their respective niches. Most people think that their passion is their niche but it is not entirely true. The best way to identify a niche is through IKIGAI. "IKIGAI" is a Japanese concept to discover one's niche. It means "reason for being".

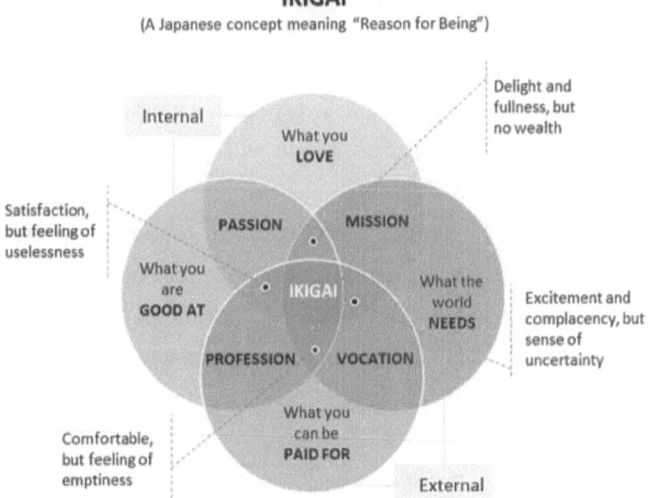

Ikigai strives to discover a niche where your passion and talent converge with the things that the world needs and is willing to pay for. Broadly it answers **"WHAT"**

Ikigai connects what's within us i.e. what we love to do and what we are good at with the external world i.e. does the world need it and is willing to pay for it. If the world is willing to pay for your niche then it means your product is creating a real value or higher perceived value. IKIGAI moment is achieved when one discovers a common answer to:

Internal
a. What you **LOVE**
b. What you are **GOOD AT**

External
c. What the world **NEEDS**
d. What you can be **PAID FOR**

Ikigai is the sweet spot at the intersection of the answers to the above questions. This sweet spot is your niche where your passion and talent converge with the things that the world needs and is willing to pay for.

You don't have to force yourself to come up with answers in one sitting. In fact, it's more productive to take some time (generally 2-4 sittings). The key is not to put pressure on yourself, allow the mind to absorb and evaluate. Keep on adding, evaluating, and editing answers.

Let us explore Ikigai through the example of Steve Jobs. We see Steve as a pioneer in technology, but that is only half a story. Primarily, Steve was a lover of fine craftsmanship as was evident from his collection of handmade Japanese teacups and flower vases. Let's imagine Steve and try to create his Ikigai.

- What you **LOVE** : Fine Craftsmanship, Art
- What you are **GOOD** at : Technology, Innovation
- What the world **NEEDS** : Smart, connected devices
- What you can be **PAID** for : Smart, connected & beautiful devices

Apple devices were mediums of his expression which the world wanted and was willing to pay for. The key lies in marrying what you love and what you are good at and looking at these from an external perspective.

Example: A person loves sharing knowledge and enjoys creating videos. His social media platforms are full of informative animated videos shot by him. Let us explore his IKIGAI moment:

- What one **LOVES** : Sharing knowledge
- What one is **GOOD** at : Shooting and editing videos
- What the world **NEEDS** : Entrepreneurs need video sales pitch to increase sales
- What one can be **PAID** for : Sharing the knowledge of shooting and editing videos

IKIGAI: He may create online tutorials on "Video secrets for High Impact Sales". Target Audience: Trainers, Business Consultants

The biggest challenge that most people face is that they are not able to marry what they love and what they are good at. This is the most critical piece. They fall victim to isolated thinking that their job, family, passion, and desires are all separate and unrelated aspects of their lives. The core of Ikigai is that nothing is isolated. Everything is connected if you have clarity on Ikigai's 4 aspects.

This realization changes the outlook for the better. Ikigai is about finding joy, fulfillment, and balance in life.

> *You can play the game and you can act out the part,*
> *even though you know it wasn't written for you.*
>
> **– James Taylor lyric**

Fish the Niche	**United Vision**	Smart Channels	Insightful Relationships

2. United Vision

> *When You Want To Succeed As Bad As You Want*
> *To Breathe, Then You Will Be Successful*
>
> **– Eric Thomas**

Ikigai answers "**What**" and Vision answers "**Why**". After identifying your niche, the next step is to look at it from a long-term perspective i.e. create a vision.

The simplest way to create a vision is to expand your niche into the future and visualize the impact that your niche could create. Vision must include your customer's ideal future state. Vision is always forward-looking and when it goes beyond self-gain it becomes united and hence more powerful.

A united vision will always inspire one to outperform his targets and milestones. It has the power to enable thoughts and decide activities which one should be doing.

Simple rules for creating a vision:
a. Forward-looking: Project your niche into the future
b. Include your customer's ideal future state
c. Look at a broader objective that is beyond self
d. Money is not the only objective, it is a by-product

Example: An entrepreneur identified his niche as a yoga teacher for senior citizens. His vision is to create a community of 100,000 healthy and happy senior citizens. This is an example of a united vision that always inspires and is a very big enabler. Some inspiring Vision statements are:

Microsoft: To help people and businesses throughout the world realize their full potential.

Nike: Bring inspiration and innovation to every athlete* in the world. (*If you have a body, you are an athlete.)

Tesla: To create the most compelling car company of the 21st century by driving the world's transition to electric vehicles.

Fish the Niche	United Vision	**Smart Channels**	Insightful Relationships

3. Smart Channels

Channels are the medium through which customers are acquired and the product reaches target customers. Channels help scale up a business. They can be of the following types:

Channel partners are your first customers and you need to create a value proposition for them to leverage their premium shelf space. New start-ups have to give in high margins and attractive payment terms to channel partners for premium space.

On the contrary, you may design a very high value proposition for end customers to create a pull in the system. Hence, channel partners will have to stock your product and then they start to lose bargaining power with you.

Example: If an entrepreneur is selling through amazon then it becomes a channel to acquire customers.

Key pointers to select the right channel:
- Explore, where your target audience is hanging out
- Offline channels are comparatively expensive than digital channels
- Always keep a track of customer acquisition cost
- When you start, prefer not to own a channel to avoid blocking up of capital
- Consider your budget and scalability goal to select a channel
- Test one new acquisition channel at a time
- Allocate part of your budget to paid channels and conduct experiments to find which ones have the highest ROI, then focus on optimizing them. Example: various social media channels, etc

Fish the Niche	United Vision	Smart Channels	**Insightful Relationships**

4. Insightful Relationships

Customer relationship serves as a communication bridge between an entrepreneur and a customer. The objective is to acquire, retain and grow customers. Carefully managed relationship reduces acquisition costs for upselling opportunities and builds a brand. It is a very important feedback mechanism and can be classified as direct or indirect.

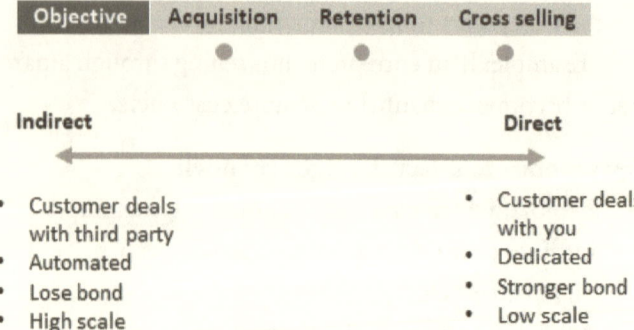

Customers always prefer dedicated support. In a small setup, entrepreneurs prefer to connect directly with the customers for a stronger bond. As the business scales up, it transitions from dedicated to automated, as per business needs. Example: Mobile operators use automated relationship management while Banks offer dedicated relationship managers for HNIs.

The components of the front force i.e. Niche, United Vision, Smart Channels, and Insightful Relationships, ensure revenue for the business which can be generated through the following 7 ways;

- One-time sale of the product,
- Usage fees,
- Subscription fees,
- Leasing fees,
- Licensing fees,
- Brokerage fees, and
- Advertising revenue

The revenue sources depend upon the type of business but one must explore the opportunity of adding up new revenue streams to make it more sustainable. Plot your revenue sources and keep a tab on cash and profit which are oxygen to keep business running and innovating.

Entrepreneurship Takeaways

- Be very clear on your front force i.e., Niche, United Vision, Smart Channels, and Insightful relationships. Front force enables revenue stream in the business model.
- Test fast, fail fast, adjust fast
- Being a perfectionist is the biggest obstacle to a startup
- Love your niche but do not get married to it
- Narrow down your niche market. Stop giving everything to everyone
- Use "Ikigai" to discover a niche where your passion and talent converge with the things that the world needs and is willing to pay for
- Expand your niche to create a vision that is beyond self
- Understand where your customers are hanging out and select the right channel to keep customer acquisition cost to the minimum
- Focus on building stronger bonds through direct connect with customers and transition them from dedicated support to automated as you scale up

9

Value Proposition

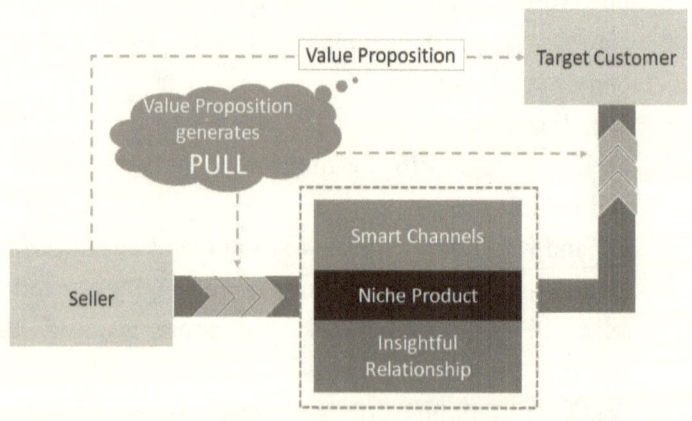

Value proposition is **the reason why a customer buys your product.** Value is the financial benefit that a customer gets in excess of the price paid. It is essentially the gap between the price paid and perceived benefits from the product. Larger the gap, higher the value. Value proposition is the compelling statement articulating specific benefits a company is offering its target market. Value proposition creates a pull in the system whereby a product is pulled off the shelf by the target customer.

How Value Proposition is designed?

Value proposition is crafted by mapping elements of customer segment i.e. A, B, C with product offering i.e. D, E, F. When a product provides a solution to a problem by killing pain or creating gain then it becomes problem-solution fit. Further, when the market accepts the solution then it finally becomes a product-market fit.

Product Offering **Customer Segment Elements**

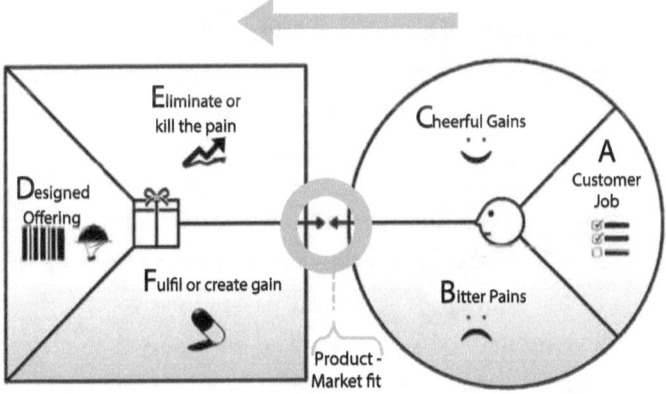

Customer Segment Elements
- **A:** A job that customer wants to do
- **B:** Bitter pains in doing the job
- **C:** Cheerful gains that customer wants

Product Offering
- **D:** Designed offering to get the job done
- **E:** Eliminate or kill the pain
- **F:** Fulfil or create gain

The product offering must enable a customer not only to effectively do the job but kill the pain and create gain. Product offering must create a value proposition in either or a combination of three categories:

Functional	Social	Emotional
• Price • Quality • Performance	• Status • Brand • Looks better	• Feel better • Emotional • Supremacy

a. Functional

Value proposition focuses on satisfying the basic reason for the product. Entrepreneurs play on performance parameters like price, quality, etc. Products leveraging functional value proposition **can not govern premium**.

Example: Ola cabs brought in the biggest disruption in the cab rental industry. Disruption simply means changing the rules of the game. Ola leveraged pay per use model vis-à-vis conventional taxi operators who earlier used to charge for at least 8 hours. Hence price became the biggest value proposition to disrupt the industry while it leveraged technology to scale up the business and provide key benefits like convenience, safety, ease of payment, etc.

Summary: This category is a no-nonsense category and comparatively easier for entrepreneurs to get in. It is meant for mass segments and the players seek to leverage price as the value proposition. The key here is to attract masses to achieve economies of scale.

b. Social

Value proposition focuses on satisfying the social status need. The customer wishes to get associated with the product and boasts off to gain social stature. Products leveraging **social value proposition govern premium**.

Example 1: High-end brands like Porsche, Ferrari, Rolex, Gucci, etc. appeal to specific target segments. The functional aspect of the product is obviously superior but the premium brand value is the value proposition.

Example 2: Cars companies leverage integration with premium brand products like boss speakers, Alexa voice control, Apple car play system, etc. to piggyback on their brand value.

Example 3: Organisations leverage the brand name of big 4 firms as auditors to establish trust during their respective IPOs.

Summary: This category requires entrepreneurs to be innovative and come up with something new frequently. There is a practical approach that is being followed here i.e. to piggyback on popular brands to create a social value proposition.

c. Emotional

Value proposition focuses on satisfying self-need to feel better. Emotion stimulates the mind 3000 times faster than rational thoughts. Products leveraging **emotional value proposition govern high premium**. These products obviously perform better on functional aspects and are meant to make a customer feel better and more confident.

Example: Parents subscribe to "Byjus" learning programs to improve their kid's knowledge and fundamentals. The subscription is not meant to boast off socially but it makes parents confident about their kid's learning.

Example: An Entrepreneur who is into the business of organic cosmetic products may create both functional and emotional value propositions. In this case, the functional quotient is obvious, as the product would serve a basic hygiene purpose but would also make a customer feel better about their skin as they are using harmless organic products.

Summary: This is the most sought-after category and requires entrepreneurs to study the target customer very closely. This requires out-of-the-box solutions to kill pain and create gain.

Any Examples of Best-in-class Value Propositions?

3 Great value proposition examples:

1. Apple MacBook

Light. Years ahead. Apple emphasizes the lightweight of its product. Secondly, the product is technologically way ahead vis-à-vis competition (competition reference is obvious). These are two value propositions communicated by apple in just three magical words i.e. Light. Years Ahead.

The differentiation which created this value proposition is the innovation in the product, which made it thin and technologically superior to the competition which leads to it being lighter and years ahead.

2. Salesforce

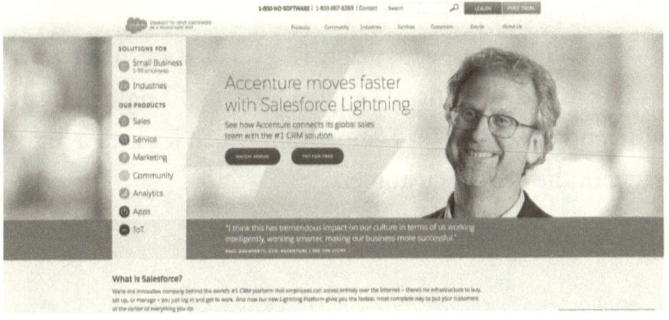

Accenture moves faster with Salesforce lightening
"Salesforce" takes a unique approach and piggybacks on one of its premium clients. In six words, it not only tells us what it does, but also introduces us to someone who can vouch for it. It sets it apart from its competition.

3. Uber

Uber has separate value propositions for drivers and riders, each one emphasizing freedom and convenience.

For riders: "**Tap your phone. Get where you're headed.**"
For drivers: **Drive when you want. Find opportunities around you**

This tells you what you need to do and what you get, even if you've never heard of Uber.

Can Differentiation Help to Create a Value Proposition?

A product that is differentiated in the eyes of the customer, will be able to create higher perceived value. When differentiation gets copied by the competition, it becomes a common factor and no longer remains a differentiator. Then you need to bring something new which changes the value proposition.

While value proposition is leveraged by front force, it is created by thrust engine. Thrust Engine creates differentiation vis-à-vis competition which leads to a higher value in the eyes of customers.

Entrepreneurship Takeaways

- Value proposition is **the reason why a customer buys your product, and not your competitor's**
- Design Value proposition that is strong enough to create a **pull in the system**
- When a start-up either kills pain or creates gain by providing a solution to the problem then it becomes a problem-solution fit. Further, when the market accepts the solution then it finally becomes a **product-market fit**
- You should start with mapping customer segment with a product offering to achieve problem-solution fit.
- Focus on achieving **social or emotional** value proposition to govern premium
- **Differentiation can be leveraged** to create higher perceived value

10

The Thrust Engine

Thrust Engine creates differentiation vis-à-vis competition which leads to a higher perceived value in the eyes of customers.

Thrust Engine means:

    a.   Essential Resources
    b.   Genius Activities
    c.   Resourceful Partnerships

I will be sharing a case study at the end of the chapter to showcase how a company can reach a leadership position by leveraging thrust engine.

a. Essential Resources

These are critical resources that must be owned for the smooth functioning of a business. These resources must be leveraged to disrupt the market and create differentiation. Essential Resources can be:

- **Financial** like a subsidized loan, angel investment, etc
- **Physical** like critical equipment, SEZ land, etc
- **Human**-like talented team members
- **Intellectual** like patents, designs, etc

A key question to ask is, what essential resources are required:

- To create Value Propositions?
- For our Smart Channels?
- For our Customer Relationships?

Example: The value proposition for Amazon is product reviews, competitive pricing, faster delivery, product range, and convenience. Essential Resources for amazon are Amazon's website, mobile app, KDP, employees, fulfillment centers, and call center that ensure value proposition for customers. The above example shows the essential resources of amazon that create its value proposition, to enable distribution channels and support customer relationships.

b. Genius Activities

Core activities that business is engaged in for the primary purpose of creating a value proposition. These activities have the power to disrupt the market. Genius activities may include operations, marketing, production, research

& development, problem-solving, and administration, depending upon the type of business. If you are an application developer, User Interface (UI) design and coding will be genius activities. On the other hand, if you are a business consultant, problem-solving can be your genius activity.

The objective is to discover activities to differentiate your product or service from your competition so that a value proposition can be created.

Example: Product reviews is one of the value proposition for Amazon. Customers gauge product performance through reviews that are missing in brick-and-mortar stores. Hence, genius activities for amazon would be all activities for creating product reviews i.e. collecting and displaying review data, merchandising, managing supply chain and logistics, etc.

c. Resourceful Partnerships

Resourceful Partnerships are the relationships that a business has with third parties like suppliers, manufacturers, etc. that help the business model work and create differentiation. It can be a strategic alliance between non-competitors, coopetition to reduce risk, joint ventures to develop businesses, and buyer-supplier relationships. The key enabler is the win-win situation for both parties.

The important point is what essential resources and genius activities are we acquiring through these partnerships. These are those resources and activities that we do not want to own.

Important questions to ask are:

- Who are our Resourceful Partners?
- Which Essential Resources are we acquiring from partners?
- Which Genius Activities do partners perform for us?

Example: If a business is selling its product on amazon then amazon is not its resourceful partner but a smart channel. Resourceful partnerships give exclusivity that helps in creating differentiation and hence create value.

Ola cabs do not own their cabs while their drivers own them. Hence, drivers are Ola's partners and their cabs are leveraged as resources.

When you start-up, prefer to avoid blocking up capital by owning resources. Try to move fixed costs to variable. Explore partnerships or outsourcing opportunities rather than creating in-house capabilities and plan phased investments as you scale up.

Thrust Engine Case Study: Ola Cabs Vis-à-vis Meru Cabs

Meru Cabs started operations in 2006 and focused on 5 components (5Cs) i.e. Customer, Company, Chauffer, Call Center, and Cab. They owned the entire fleet of cabs. Drivers were hired who paid a fixed daily subscription fee to Meru, basically, drivers were franchisees. Meru supported drivers through the call center to push leads to them. Hence, the onus was on drivers to make money and pay-back Meru its rent.

This model is nothing new, Meru just re-did the age-old concept. Many cabs and auto-rickshaws on the roads are actually owned by someone else who rents out the vehicle to a driver. The driver pays a certain amount as a daily rent. Post all the expenses like rentals, fuel, etc., the driver pockets remaining as his day's earnings. So instead of doing things on a small scale, Meru stepped in and played on a larger scale.

Ola which started in 2010 aggregated cars from taxi operators or individuals. Here, drivers owned the cars and they worked for Ola. In addition to 5Cs, Ola focused on technology as well. Ola connected customers with driver partners through a mobile app.

Even after starting 4 years late, Ola was able to scale up quickly and surpassed Meru. In 2019, Ola had a market share of 56% vis-à-vis 2% for Meru. The value proposition for Ola was very clear i.e. being affordable and hassle-free for customers. This proposition was achieved through technology which was the biggest differentiator. While Meru had a large call center team to pick orders and coordinate between driver and customer, Ola leveraged the mobile application to their advantage.

Cabs were the essential resources for Meru as they own their fleet while mobile app was the essential resource for Ola which was the biggest differentiator that created value proposition of being affordable and hassle-free.

Entrepreneurship Takeaways

- Be very clear on differentiation which enables value proposition. Explore differentiation through elements

of thrust engine i.e., Essential Resources, Genius Activities and Resourceful Partnerships.
- Essential Resources are to be owned for creating a value proposition, or for distribution channels, or to support customer relationship
- Identify genius activities to disrupt the market
- Ensure stringent upkeep of essential resources and monitoring of genius activities
- Explore resourceful partners for leveraging resources and activities that you do not want to own
- Resourceful partnerships can be leveraged for scaling up

11

It's *Different*

> *There is no such thing as a commodity.*
> *It is simply a product waiting to be differentiated.*
>
> – Philip Kotler

After a series of successful projects across the country whose case studies were shared globally, it was during the best of these times my career took one more turn.

I got an opportunity to head the strategy function of India's largest construction equipment company, JCB India Ltd. It gave me a lifetime opportunity to participate in board room discussions with eminent industry leaders to design and implement market leadership strategies. Here, I had walked the journey to grow and sustain the market leadership position.

Technologies change, methods change and ways to connect also change but the focus of giving a differentiated experience to the customer remains at the core of a market leader. The biggest differentiator is to create sustained value to make customers' businesses successful.

How Differentiation creates Value Proposition

Designing Differentiation is an art and a science. Here are 11 chosen examples to depict the same.

1. The "X" factor:

"Be an Expert" on something in the industry i.e. **Outperform competition** on at least one dimension.

Example 1: Royal Enfield is a synonym for retro-style leisure biking in India. The design of the bike is the key differentiator, which follows its brand positioning of being a leisure bike. The value proposition for the customer is the driving experience that is social and emotional.

Example 2: Domino's may not talk about its products but it definitely conveys its guaranteed delivery within 30 minutes. The entire front-end and back-end operations are designed to deliver orders accordingly.

The process design across the value chain is the differentiator and value proposition is 30 minutes delivery.

The above two examples depict, how brand positioning impacts differentiation that leads to a value proposition.

2. Hook & Bait

Make it easier for the customer to buy the basic product, make customer addicted to the product and leverage upsell opportunities for complementary or refill products.

Example: Gillette Mach 3 razor is a premium product and it gives a free blade with every razor. The differentiator is the premium razor with a blade in a combo package at a reasonable price. An attractive product clubbed with an irresistible offer is an emotional value proposition that pulls us toward a purchase. In a few days, the blade becomes blunt and we are left with no choice but to buy expensive Gillette blades as no other blade will fit into the razor. Hence for Gillette, the razor is a one-time revenue while blades are a recurring revenue source. Similarly, other combinations include printer – inkjet cartridges, Roller pens – refills, software – AMC, etc.

3. Niche Products

Niche products have a built-in brand differentiation. They satisfy the specific demands of a typical type of customer at a premium.

Example: Hand-crafted wooden toys are a niche segment. These toys work on basic mechanics and are considered safe for kids. The target customers are parents who value skill and craftsmanship. Hence they are willing to pay a premium over factory-made plastic toys

The differentiation is the hand-crafted wood and the value proposition is the safety aspect for kids. Hence one needs to fish the niche and leverage it as a differentiator to govern premium.

4. Disruptive Pricing

Innovative marketers create a dummy product and use it to create an imaginary reference point for customers. Customers perceive a higher value in the actual product being offered than the dummy product.

Example 1: A start-up is into publishing economy research magazines. It is an annual subscription-based model. They innovatively price their product, as under:

Annual Subscription Price: 12 monthly magazines

1. Hard Copy: Rs. 24,000
2. Soft Copy: Rs. 8,000
3. Hard + Soft Copy: Rs. 24,100

Clearly, option 1 is a dummy option as it gives customers a higher perceived value in option 3. In the absence of Option 1, option 2 would have been a preferred choice.

This pricing creates a double impact by increasing value per unit by pushing customers from option 2 to option 3 and sales volume as well.

In a competitive environment, you need to always focus on selling the value. The more you focus on the value, the less important the price becomes.

> *"Don't ever sell cheap, even if you have to, sell value"*
>
> – SMR

5. Unique Buying Experience

A memorable buying experience can be a big differentiator. Create an effortless experience and end the buying cycle with a pleasant surprise for the customer.

Example: There are emerging start-ups trying their hands in multi-brand car service stations. The pain that they are trying to solve is:

   a. Expensive car servicing at authorized car dealerships
   b. Lack of transparency in work being done if one goes to unauthorized service stations

We get service reminders from start-ups to kill the pain and create gain by offering:

- Value service packages
- Free pick-up and drop
- You can see your car getting serviced
- Easy connect with the service manager
- When the car comes back after service, the bill value is always lower than the quoted price
- The car comes back with a free branded gift
- Payment is through an online link which is hassle-free
- Going forward their CRM team grows this relationship to make us a loyal customer

The value proposition is transparency in pricing that builds trust. Further, free services like pick-up and drop, branded gift, etc. have become a norm and customers always love certainty.

This is a classic example of a unique buying experience but it works only when it is backed by a superior product or service performance.

6. Innovation

Innovation is always a very strong differentiator and takes the value proposition to emotional levels.

Example: Lately, some start-ups are venturing into organic farming. The value proposition for customers is pesticide-free organic fruits and vegetables. The differentiators are the use of organic manure and paper packaging of the final produce. The initial challenge was the cost to the customer, which was higher as compared to conventional vegetables at local markets. The start-ups are now innovating in this domain by:

1. Applying hydroponic farming technique that uses mineral-rich water instead of soil. This gives flexibility in crop selection and also enables economies of scale
2. Vertical farming improves space utilization by cultivating crops one over the other in a vertical stack structure design, thereby giving more produce per square foot
3. Aggregating organic producers to achieve economies of scale

Hence the crop becomes economically viable with improved quality.

7. Old wine in a new bottle

This is an old proven technique and the key is to create differentiation with innovative packaging and unique branding styles to create a new perceived value.

Example: There is a famous eatery brand in India that operates on a "delivery only model". Recently, they changed their entire packaging concept from plastic disposables to earthen pots. It has been able to create differentiation with earthen pots. The value being added to the customer is emotional as they perceive earthen pots to be a healthier option than plastic cutlery.

Hence we have to figure out what clicks with our target customer and leverage it.

8. Customer-centricity, a real differentiator

Something that makes life easier for customers, will make it more desirable than the competition.

Example: The vision statement of Amazon says it all, "to be Earth's most customer-centric company…" The processes are customer friendly and super easy to navigate like product reviews, shopping, delivery, tracking, refunds, returns, customer service, etc. This has generated a bond of trust and has positioned Amazon as a real customer-centric company.

Example: Customer-centricity with multiple customers. At times, there are multiple customers. JCB, a market leader in construction equipment, serves 3 distinct customers:

a. **Financier**, who wants the owner of the machine, to earn from it and pay back installments in time
b. **Owner**, who leases out the equipment to operator and looks for higher fuel efficiency and lower running cost
c. **Operator**, who is mostly a first-time entrepreneur and looks for higher productivity and ease of operation to complete the work in the least amount of time

All three customers have different yardsticks. JCB leverages emotional value proposition to excite different categories of customers, as:

Financier: Payback-period, Resale Value
Owner: Fuel Efficiency, Resale Value, Telematics, Lifecycle cost
Operator: Machine performance, Ergonomic design
Creating win-win: Over the years, JCB has become a platform for promoting entrepreneurship at the grass-root level. It celebrates the journey of customers graduating from operators to owners. It has changed the game to own and operate a machine through its wide distribution network, ease of financing, technology, training schools etc. It has resulted in creating a **win-win** situation for all stakeholders.

9. Limit Availability

Limiting the availability by leveraging time or quantity can help to increase perceived value. When customers perceive that everyone will not be able to own the product, perceived value and the demand increases.

Example 1: Limited day sales on an e-commerce website like "Big Billion days" sales etc. pull customers for the fear of losing out on lucrative deals.

Example 2: Special editions of cars (like anniversary, festive editions etc.) sell like hot cake with higher premiums. It has a more social value quotient.

10. Secure the future: It is not always about the product

Products are bought with the future in mind. Understand the core challenges of the target customer and offer a solution that is actually or may seem customized. If we are able to secure the future in the mind of the customer then the objective is achieved.

Example: There are budding businesses that offer money-back or replacement with a tagline "*No questions asked*" or buy-back schemes. Customers feel secure in doing business with them. Some fat loss equipment are sold with the promise of stated results, provided the customer follows exercise and diet routine. In case customers do not get results, they promise 100% money back with "No questions asked".

11. Brand Story

A brand should have a story, not of its own but a customer story narrated by the brand. Customer story will seamlessly connect the target market with the brand i.e. they will start owning the brand. The brand story has the power to make a brand much larger than life.

Example: "Nike" is much larger than its product, it is not about shoes but about connecting people emotionally with sports personalities. Customers get inspired by the stories of legends depicting their hard work, passion, and overcoming failures. The differentiator is establishing connect with people and the value proposition is truly emotional i.e. inspiring people to perform. The message is very clear that if they can do it, you too can, hence their tag line "Just do it"

> *Never start a business just to make money, start a business to make a difference*
>
> **– Marie Forleo**

Entrepreneurship Takeaways

- The focus of an entrepreneur should be to build a Brand by creating differentiation which will ensure a true value proposition
- Out of the box thinking also helps design differentiation
- Brand positioning impacts differentiation i.e. "X factor" differentiation will have a premium positioning vis-à-vis "disruptive pricing"
- Differentiation has the power to disrupt the market and change the game. One needs to figure out:

    a. The right type of differentiation (as shared in the above 11 examples)

b. The right way i.e. how differentiation is to be achieved in the selected type i.e. identify front force and thrust engine to achieve differentiation

PHASE 4

Start-Up Shastra

12

Startup Shastra

An entrepreneurial mindset is about conviction in your ideas and clarity in business model i.e. Front force, value proposition, and thrust engine. A professional in a job can do wonders if he/she thinks like an entrepreneur. This mindset

has helped me enormously to think about solutions in the job and create my value proposition. One needs to explore the micro-niche like being a data specialist, digital expert, execution master, etc. Your strength is your differentiator that creates your brand value proposition. You can leverage thrust engine i.e. resources, genius activities and develop partnerships with colleagues to strengthen your value proposition.

Also, entrepreneurship has nothing to do with age. The best example for us is Colonel Sanders who founded KFC at the age of 62. Some people are driven by a dream to do something transformational for themselves and society. I am still evolving as an entrepreneur, it is an exciting, never-ending journey. The most critical element is to find one's niche. No one stops you from exploring your niche when you are 40 +. Actually, your niche does not know your age.

> *Never too young to start an empire.*
> *Never too old to chase a new dream*
>
> **– Anonymous**

Over the last 20 years, I have been part of various startup journeys as an entrepreneur, investor, and coach. I have been guiding entrepreneurs, students of MBA colleges on business modelling for their start-ups, and have coached my spouse to launch her start-up on science-based kits for kids. These all learnings have been summarized in the form of Start-up Shastra **comprising of 15 sutras**, coined as an acronym:

"INCLUSIVE GROWTH"

1. **I:** **I**dea Generation
2. **N:** **N**iche
3. **C:** **C**ustomer
4. **L:** **L**everage Systems
5. **U:** **U**nited Vision
6. **S:** **S**mart Channels
7. **I:** **I**nsightful Relationships
8. **V:** **V**alue Proposition
9. **E:** **E**ssential Resources
10. **G:** **G**enius Activities
11. **R:** **R**esourceful Partnership
12. **O:** **O**utclass Competition
13. **W:** **W**inning Team
14. **T:** **T**horough your Finances
15. **H:** **H**ook & Nudge

Startup Shastra is a structure that guides you throughout your startup journey and answers your fundamental queries. If you want to start and are confused about what, how, and where to start then the first Sutra i.e. Idea generation will help you bring clarity. If you already have an idea, then the second sutra i.e. Niche, will guide you towards exploring your niche through Ikigai, seeding and testing the product. These 15 sutras have been discretely elaborated in previous chapters and are now summarized as:

1. Idea Generation

- Look at the problem from GOD's perspective (GOD: Generator, Operator, Destroyer)

- An idea should solve a problem (kill pain or create gain)
- Design WIFM to create buy-in for your ideas
- Our Mind is an Engine of Ideas and It is very important to know what TO DO but more important to figure out what NOT TO DO
- Being a perfectionist is the biggest obstacle to a startup

2. Niche

- Explore your niche through "Ikigai", where your passion and talent converge with the things that the world needs and is willing to pay for
- Love your niche but don't get married to it
- Test fast, fail fast, adjust fast
- Seed and test your idea with the smaller but real customers, even before you get your final product in shape. This will help to refine your niche, if required
- Categorize your offerings into Base, Core, and Premium products for upsell opportunities with sustained customer value at the core

3. Customer

- Focus on creating sustained customer value
- Narrow down your niche market
- If you are targeting everybody, you are targeting nobody
- Preempt and design the meeting flow. Use CLOVE to prepare well for key meetings to achieve designed outcomes

- Product is king but engagement is queen, and the lady rules the house

4. Leverage Systems

- Systems work, People network
- Systems are the backbone for consistent customer experience.
- Entrepreneurs should focus on creating systems to make things simple and fast for customers by putting repeatable tasks on autopilot mode while people are to be leveraged to network, innovate, execute and lead
- "A place for everything and everything in its place" is the first step to put operations on Auto-pilot mode

5. United Vision

- Should answer the need for the existence
- Expand your niche to create a vision that is beyond self
- Vision must include your customer's ideal future state
- Focus on a larger cause and should be forward-looking

6. Smart Channels

- Explore, where your target audience is hanging out and select the right channel to keep customer acquisition cost to the minimum
- When you start, prefer not to own a channel to avoid blocking up of capital
- Consider your budget and scalability goal to select a channel
- Test one new acquisition channel at a time

- Channel partners are your first customers. Hence, create a value proposition for channel partners as well, to leverage their premium shelf space
- A higher value proposition for end customers creates pull in the system. Hence, channel partners will have to stock your product and then they will lose bargaining power over you
- Allocate part of your budget to paid channels and conduct experiments to find which ones have the highest ROI, then focus on optimizing them

7. Insightful Relationships

- A very important feedback mechanism
- A tool to acquire, retain and grow customers
- Carefully managed relationship reduces acquisition cost for upselling opportunities and builds brand
- Focus on building stronger bonds through direct connect with customers and transition them from dedicated support to automated as you scale up

8. Value Proposition

- It is the reason why a customer buys your product
- Focus on achieving social or emotional value proposition to govern premium
- When a start-up either kills pain or creates gain by providing a solution to the problem then it becomes a problem-solution fit. Further, when the market accepts the solution then it finally becomes a product-market fit.
- You should start with mapping customer segment with a product offering to achieve problem-solution fit

- Differentiation can be leveraged to create higher perceived value

9. Essential Resources

- Essential Resources are to be owned for creating a value proposition, or for distribution channels, or to support customer relationship
- Identify essential resources from the list of resources. All resources are not essential. Start with "must-have" resources to minimize investment
- Ensure stringent upkeep of these resources

10. Genius Activities

- Critically evaluate activities that create value proposition
- Genius activities have a high potential of designing differentiation to disrupt the market
- Ensure stringent monitoring of genius activities
- Innovate to bring pleasant customer experiences

11. Resourceful Partnerships

- Explore resourceful partners for leveraging their resources and activities which you do not want to own
- These partners give you exclusivity and hence are different from vendors
- Leverage these partnerships for scaling up

12. Outclass Competition

- A product that is differentiated in the eyes of the customer, will be able to create higher perceived value

- The key is to focus on creating higher value for the customer vis-à-vis competition
- When differentiation gets copied by the competition, it becomes a common factor and no longer remains a differentiator. Then you need to bring something new which changes the value proposition
- Competitive positioning forms the basis for designing differentiation. For Example: "X factor" differentiation will have a premium positioning vis-à-vis "disruptive pricing"
- Don't ever sell cheap, even if you have to, sell value
- "Begin with the end in mind" is the most powerful way to get the thinking engine on the right track
- Never let any condition put you inside a box. If you are non-decisive; try to see the Box, Just remove it
- When everything falls apart and you cannot see an opportunity, create it. Entrepreneurs don't wait for an opportunity, they create it
- Thinking with a broader perspective and leveraging the resources and situation at hand can covert risk into an opportunity

13. Winning Team

- Design WIFM to create buy-in
- Energise team with a clear vision and plan to transform
- Evaluate people from the perspective of ASK (Attitude, Skill and Knowledge) and their efforts to increase the area of ASK triangle. Expertise is important but Positive Attitude is paramount.
- Use ATM to gauge the attitude of people

- Develop employees as essential resources to create a value proposition

14. Thorough your Finances

- Just like niche, be very clear on revenue streams on day 1 which can be generated in 7 ways; one-time sale of the product, usage fees, subscription fees, leasing fees, licensing fees, brokerage fees, and advertising revenue.
- When you start-up, always avoid blocking up capital by owning resources. Try to move fixed costs to variable. For example: Explore partnerships or outsourcing opportunities rather than creating in-house capabilities, explore digital distribution channels than physical to minimize the initial cost of investment. Hence it is critical to look at essential resources, genius activities, resourceful partnerships, smart channels, and insightful relationships and plan phased investments as you scale up
- Cash and Profit are oxygen to keep business running and innovating
- Your business plan can impress an investor if there is:
    - Strong conviction in the idea
    - Genuinely solves a problem
    - Potential to scale up
    - Clarity in the business model
    - Creates value proposition
    - Strength of winning team
    - Needless to say, sustainable & profitable

15. Hook & Nudge:

Focus on 5 pointers for overcoming initial resistance

- Start nimble
- Take it to the last mile
- It is not about perfection, you can improve your game every-day
- Focusing on a larger cause will keep you motivated
- To steer the final nudge, get yourself hooked in a way that you cannot run away. Overthinking in the pursuit of perfectionism or fear of failure leads to analysis-paralysis. A simple workaround is getting hooked. A simple hook can be like committing a launch date, getting your skin in the game by investing effort and money

100 trending startups in 10 categories

I have encapsulated over 100 trending start-up niches that are evolving under 10 domains:

1. Health and Wellness (16)

Yoga Trainer, Stress management counsellors, Spiritual healer, Fitness Apps, Health foods, Health supplements (multivitamins), Meditation experts (Vipassana, Music therapy), Precision Medicine, Immunity boosters, Organic supplements, Herbs & juices, Innovative exercise equipment, Yoga essentials, Wellness equipment, Preventive health checkup labs, Natural treatments (Ayurveda, Acupuncture, Acupressure, etc)

2. Business Growth (17)

Business analytics for corporates, Artificial Intelligence & Machine Learning, Product specialists, Tax & Compliance consultants (compliance & audit), Operational efficiency specialists (equipment & training), Strategy consultant, Safety compliance (equipment & training), Digital agencies, Social media experts, Brand Logo specialists, e-commerce platforms, CRM agencies, Digital printers, corporate gifts, Research magazines, Channel partners (offline & online), packaging designers

3. Career growth (10)

Business analytics trainers, Artificial Intelligence, Cloud computing, Subject matter experts (Lean, Six Sigma, etc.), System experts, Business communication, Leadership training, Career counselor, Recruitment consultants, Skill upgrade centers

4. Online money making (12)

Affiliate marketing, Online re-sellers, Drop-shipping, Product photography & editing for e-commerce, Stock research, Digital marketing, social media influencers, Freelancers, Blogging, Online courses, podcasting, copywriting

5. Food & Beverages (11)

App-based delivery only models, Cloud Kitchen, Nutritional foods, Innovative Chocolates, Specialty restaurants, food e-carts, QSR (Quick service restaurants at petrol pumps, airports, malls, etc), packaged foods (tofu, cheese, etc.), ready to eat packaged food, food equipment (griller, commercial ovens), food equipment AMCs

6. Farming (11)

Organic farming, hydroponic farming, Vertical farming, Speciality farming (mushroom, ginger, etc.), Exotic plants, Oxygen plants, Horticulture, Seeds, Organic nutrients (nitrogen sticks), Cocopeat bricks, Vermicompost

7. Environment (15)

E-vehicles assembly, E-vehicles infrastructure support (charging stations), Battery design & integration, Traffic management software, Water purifiers (from the environment, sea, etc.), Vertical gardens (Equipment, training, and AMC), Micro foresting, Waste recycling, Products from wastes, Pollution monitoring equipment, pollution control equipment (Air filters, Air quality monitors, etc.), Paper bags, paper gift packaging, Recycled paper seed pencils, paper disposable cutlery

8. Art & Craft (4)

Designer pots and planters (cement, gypsum, etc), Handicrafts online trading, Designer Imitation jewellery, fashion accessories

9. Relationships (6)

Parenting (kids, teen, adult), Marriage proposals, Marriage counsellors, Adoption, Mid-life crisis, Elderly care (equipment & support service)

10. Consolidators (4)

Milk consolidators, Farm produce consolidators, Restaurant consolidators, Car & Bike service consolidators

> *97% of the people who quit too soon are employed by the 3% who never gave up*
>
> **– Anonymous**

A Well-Deserved Gift: FREE E-book on 7 Steps Startup System

Congratulations on completing the book. As a gesture to honour your investment in time and efforts, you are entitled for a **FREE E-book** on 7 Steps Startup System. It is a step-by-step guide for aspiring Entrepreneurs with solutions to practical challenges. You can download the book at **www.art2start.in**

Further, you also have an opportunity to register for my upcoming webinars specifically designed for children to **THINK OUT OF THE BOX**. The program is very focused and one can see the positive outcome in just 2 hours. You can register for the program at www.art2start.in.

A Big Thankyou &
A Humble Request

Finally, I would like to heartily thank you for keeping your faith in a debutant writer. I hope you have enjoyed the read and taken back some actionable insights.

As I am young at writing, that's why I try much harder to differentiate and give you real value. Startup shastra is the gist of my 20 years of learning. If I have been able to add value, I'd appreciate if you could leave a review of the book on amazon. Your kind efforts will help me immensely to build trust and grow my readership.

Your review is oxygen for me to support lifeline ☺
Thank you and have a successful entrepreneurial journey!!

www.ingramcontent.com/pod-product-compliance
Lightning Source LLC
Chambersburg PA
CBHW030807180526
45163CB00003B/1173